native american identities

native

american

identities

Scott B. Vickers

FROM STEREOTYPE

TO ARCHETYPE

IN ART AND

LITERATURE

University of New Mexico Press
Albuquerque

Dedicated to the memory of my mother,
Adelle, and father, William, whose passion
for learning and generosity of spirit
inspired me always, and to my other
human and animal allies, especially Mark,
Luke, Molly, Alexander, and Fanny

For Frank Waters, whose kiva-like heart
gracefully entertained the gods
of a civilization not his own

Library of Congress Cataloging-in-Publication Data
Vickers, Scott B., 1947–
Native American identities : from stereotype to archetype in art
and literature / Scott B. Vickers. — 1st ed.
p   cm.
Includes bibliographical references and index.
ISBN 0-8263-1931-9 (cloth). — ISBN 0-8263-1886-X (pbk.)
1. Indians of North America—Ethnic identity.   2. Indians in
literaure.   3. Indians in art.   4. Indians of North American—
Cultural assimilation.   5. Stereotype (Psychology)   I. Title.
E98.E85V53   1998
305.897—dc21   98-9993
                          CIP

contents

acknowledgments

The inspiration for researching, writing, and compiling this manuscript has come from many diverse resources and people whose contributions I would like now to acknowledge. I hope this work will repay in some part their financial, professional, and emotional support. My parents, Bill and Adelle, have given me immense encouragement and support during all of my academic career, and I hope they are at last thankful that I have finished something I started; I only wish that my mother had lived to see its publication. Professor Kent Casper and the Humanities Department at the University of Colorado at Denver were generous enough to award me two tuition grants toward the completion of the original manuscript, as well as showing genuine concern for my academic livelihood. I am also indebted to Professor Charles Moone and Bradford Mudge of the University of Colorado at Denver, and to Professor Paul Zolbrod of Allegheny College, for their advice and reading of this manuscript during its various manifestations, for which they have received no compensation but its publication. I am indebted to Atlatl, a Phoenix resource group for those researching Indian artists, for providing me access to those whose illustrations are included in this book, and to Hachivi Edgar Heap of Birds, Jaune Quick-to-See Smith, and Diego Romero for providing the works themselves.

I would also like to thank Tom and Marilyn Auer and Michael Evans-Smith of *The Bloomsbury Review* for introducing me to the rich world of modern multicultural literature and for ideas and resources they have provided during my research. Bob Nauman, a doctoral candidate at the University of New Mexico, was instrumental in helping me find a focus for the discussion and has been an inspiration and resource on Indian artists and the history of Indian art. Barbara Guth, my editor at the University of New Mexico Press, has given me every chance to make this book as good as it could be, so I must bear full responsibility for any failings herein. Above all, I would like to thank my longtime companion, Mark Waddell, for making considerable personal and financial sacrifices that I might reach this watermark in my life. I say with all humility that I could not have done it without all of their support, encouragement, and love.

preface

As an editor of a book review magazine, I have been an observer of the shifting focuses of the publishing world for the last five years. During this time there has been a phenomenal increase in the number of books by and about Native Americans or on Native American subjects. New critical works on Native writing have proliferated, as have anthologies covering both emerging and established Indian writers. A few Indian novelists and poets have gained unheard-of, and long overdue, support from their publishers in terms of book contracts and promotional expenses, and new Indian writers are being signed more frequently by major houses. Native artists, even those outside the mainstream, continue to gain wider audiences and national attention from museums and collectors. Beautifully produced books of Native American art, both traditional and contemporary, are more widely available now than ever before.

At the same time, and perhaps for the same reasons, the mainstream American media outside of publishing have shown an interest in new movies, plays, documentaries, and journalistic endeavors relating to Indian life. Ted Turner Enterprises produced a serious documentary series and accompanying book called *The Native Americans*, which received high critical acclaim and favorable market shares. The film *Dances with Wolves* was hailed as the most Indian-centered motion picture ever made, and its huge success prompted its producer and star, actor Kevin Costner, to create his own documentary series about Native Americans. Other recent films, such as *The Black Robe*, *The Mission*, *Thunderheart*, *The Deerslayer*, and even Disney Studios' animated *Pocahontas*, all represent an upsurge in interest about Indian themes and Indian peoples, together with an accompanying marketability that is sure to produce more such interest.

Perhaps the much-maligned notions of "political correctness" and "multiculturalism" can be credited with producing new audiences for Native Americana, whether on the level of mass-media entertainment or on that of a more committed regard for cross-cultural understanding and rapprochement. Perhaps mainstream America has realized, as well, the immense potentialities and responsibilities that have been its heritage all along as a nation of diverse, and increasingly fragmented, ethnic, cultural, and religious components. I have come to hope, in the writing of this work, that there is a distinct possibility for the political and religious powers that be to understand, finally, that the responsible claims of Native Americans, as well as those of all other ethnic and religious minorities, can and must be addressed on a national level.

The writers and artists I have chosen to discuss have, in part, been chosen because of their sociopolitical concerns and their commitments both inside and outside of their particular art form, as well as for the aesthetics that contain their messages. All three of the non-Indian writers discussed in detail—Helen Hunt Jackson, Oliver La Farge, and Frank Waters—for instance, devoted many years of their adult lives not only to writing about Indians but also to lobbying Congresses and presidents of the United States on Indian affairs, serving on national associations both governmental and nongovernmental whose causes were pro-Indian and pro–human rights, and generally actively supporting the cause of Indian survival and sovereignty. They did so at a time when everything hung in the balance, and in many important ways helped create or influence the significant turn in Indian affairs that occurred at the outset of the Franklin D. Roosevelt administration in 1933, however controversial that turn might seem to us in the 1990s.

A number of the Indian artists and writers I profile have spoken and still do speak out eloquently for activism, political and economic justice, and their rights as indigenous peoples; several also serve their homelands and their people through community service, teaching, and advocacy. In many ways, to speak of contemporary Indian art and literature without taking note of their political messages is to miss the point entirely. All said, as an author and editor I have been unable and unwilling, on account of my research and experience, to extract from this discussion its obvious political undertones: concerns that continue today behind the literary and artistic scenes, on every reservation and in the hearts and minds of modern Indians, and on the national political front, whose vicissitudes continue to endanger the welfare of indigenous peoples. This is a book about identity, which cannot exist in a political vacuum or without economic viability.

It is also a book about history, which is always about politics and state-certified religion. The history of images by and about Indians is one derived from the imaginative insinuations of several centuries of conquest and colonialism; but images *about* Indians have traditionally precluded those *by* Indians, and have largely been written by the hand of the conqueror. In the Americas, the very existence of "alien races" of indigenous peoples provided a hoard of images that both beguiled and bedeviled the conquering imagination. Even today, non-Indians frequently adopt or co-opt Native American iconography and cosmogenic narratives as artistic or literary playthings, with little regard for their original significance within Native life. What this book hopes to rectify, if only in a small way, is the perception that Native cultures exist solely for the exploitation and entertainment of non-Indian audiences, and that what Indians themselves have to say about their existence and identities is thereby somehow beside the point. While the following discussion does reiterate, in the interest of historical and scholarly background, the research and observations of many who have gone before regarding the cataloguing of various images of the Indian, I hope that it also transcends this legacy by providing detailed discussions of writers and artists whose contributions to a new attitude toward Indians, and thus a new public perception of their various cultures, have heretofore been largely overlooked. The colonial mind-set still plows ahead, leaving in its wake a repertoire of image-borne fantasies and political realities that must now be honestly dealt with before they can be completely forgotten. I leave it for readers to decide how that end is best pursued, and advise them that this work itself contributes to the system of representation of Indian identities already in print. As such, it should prove useful only as a guide to deeper inquiries into the nature of living Native peoples.

native american identities

It seems native peoples' histories have been ignored and replaced by the myths of historians. This is not acceptable.

Joanna Osburn Bigfeather, Cherokee artist, "Artists Who Are Indians"

To accept the white man's religion with all the strain of new habits and beliefs, an Indian almost had to feel like a white man and have a white man's history. Instead, he longed for new life, colored by Indian history, to come into the Indian religion.

Ruth Underhill, ethnologist

The issue of human identity has always been intertwined with "histories" of different kinds: personal psychic history, genealogical family history, "tribal" history associated with ethnic and/or racial origins, sociopolitical history, ideological or cultural history involved with the development of so-called points of view or world views, the history of human origins in general (whether mythological or scientific), and ultimately cosmological history that is personified by a deity or deities who may or may not be involved intimately with human identity. How such histories are conceived, lived out, and passed on from person to person and from generation to generation inevitably involves the use of language, whether written, oral, or pictorial, and thus identity can be seen as a linguistic construct of some sort. As the biblical Gospel of John states, "In the beginning was the Word, and the Word was with God, and the Word was God," a passage that establishes a vivid link between language and the ultimate identity, that of God the creator. In the process by which individuals and cultures seek their identity, language thus plays a supremely powerful role as both the bearer and creator of all histories.

What, then, can Joanna Bigfeather mean when she says that "native peoples' histories have been ignored," that they have been supplanted by the "myths of historians"? The answer lies in the plasticity of signification inherent in language, and in the way different histories are told in vastly different languages. The foundational "Word" that "was God" for John is not the same word that signifies God for Joanna Bigfeather. John's word "was made flesh" in the person of Christ, and, as written language, made palpable and reproducible. For non-Christian cultures, those that do not have a mythological history based on the biblical word, the word that is God was made flesh, or became incarnate symbolically, in an immense diversity of other manifestations.

North American Indian cultures evolved without a written language; their traditions and their relationships with their gods were communicated orally and pictorially as creation legends and elaborately imaginative stories and songs. Thus the ultimate identities of Native Americans, as assumed through their emulation or projection of the identities of their god(s), are based on histories that have little to do with the word of John or the racial history and exclusive litany of the Bible. Personal and cultural identities, then, become linguistically and semiologically attached to the meanings behind the words for God, meanings whose very nature can be ignored, permuted, denigrated, "written over" (in the sense of a palimpsest), or even obliterated by other meanings, other Words. Because identity relies so heavily on the significance of a combination of linguistically transmitted histories, it is somewhat precarious and subject to the intrusion or influence of other histories, other identities. Unless individuals act to retain their personal and cultural histories, as they perceive them, they can face an insignificance that presages their very extinction, as has nearly been the case with the indigenous peoples of the Americas.

In the discussion that follows, I will address the way language in various forms acts as both a destroyer and a creator of identity. As the guiding mythos of the colonial cultures of white Euramerica, Christianity, both as a linguistic construct and a political force, has sought to destroy the historical identities of Indian cultures and individuals. In collusion with the political imperatives of colonialism, Christians and Christian societies have created numerous self-perpetuating stereotypes of Indians that, because they have submerged Indian histories, have sought both to void Indians of any viable sense of identity with their own cultures, mythologies, or even individuals, and also to inject in their stead the "whiteness" endemic to Christian culture and identity. American Indians, having no traditional written language, have had to contend with the Christian "Word of God" largely on an intuitive, political, and ceremonial level. Their history over the last five hundred years has literally been written by the dominating culture, and this writing has replaced and obscured the oral and pictorial histories by which Indians knew themselves during the centuries before contact. Consequently, contemporary Indians have become a tragically conflicted people, living between the two worlds of their own historical culture and that of Christian America. Some have found singular identities that rely on a deft adaptation and manipulation of both these worlds. As Flathead-Salish artist Jaune Quick-to-See Smith has noted, "I was born a redskin, raised an Indian, and now I'm a Native American, an indigenous person, a 'skin,' or a citizen of an Indian nation." "Each one of these names," observes art critic Lucy Lippard, "had and has historical significance; each is applied from outside or inside according to paternalistic, parental, or personal experience."[1]

The distinction Lippard makes between "outside" and "inside" is crucial to the discussion at hand, for it highlights a parallel distinction between objective and subjective identity. Throughout this argument I will bring into play a bipolar differentiation between stereotypes, which construct identity from the "outside," or objectively, and archetypes, which construct identity from the "inside," or subjectively; these two concepts deserve some definition at the outset. During the last five hundred years of colonial expansion in what is now called the United States, what Indians have long considered to be their heterogeneous identities (for each Indian tribe has developed its own tribal identity) have slowly and methodically been re-structured, by "the myths of historians," into a more homogenous identity that groups all Indians into a single amalgamated "tribe." This amalgama-tion has been accomplished by the "outside" influences of the colonizing culture, whose goal has been "the delirious illusion of uniting the world under the aegis of a single principle—that of a homogeneous substance of the Jesuits of the Counter Reformation," as Jean Baudrillard has suggested, or, in the United States, that of Puritan Protestantism, Catholicism, Mor-monism, Mennonitism, and various other religious agencies.[2] In accom-plishing this end, it has been necessary to create a single Indian entity out of many, a process that has in turn necessitated the formulation of stereotypes that replace historical Indian identities with an easily manipulated same-ness. At the level of theocracy, this translation of the Indian has largely been effected through a systematic denial of Indian religious and cultural heritages and a simultaneous indoctrination into Christianized mythology and dogma. As we shall see, this "conversion" has met with considerable resistance, as it has in most all colonized cultures, that has in turn sanctioned the use of military, legal, and political forces to marginalize traditional Indian identities not only theologically but physically and economically as well. That this conversion has been implemented through a racial ideology, a collusion of mythopoesis and racism, is the main topic of this discussion.

WHAT CONSTITUTES A STEREOTYPE?

The images that have been projected onto American Indians from the "outside" fall into two distinct categories: one "positive" (that of the Noble Savage) and one "negative" (that of the Ignoble Savage). The various subgroups within these two categories are delineated in chapter 3, but as an introduction, I would suggest the following criteria by which the supposed "racial inferior," in this case the American Indian, can be and has been stereotyped.

Conditions of the "Positive" Stereotype
The affected group is:

> glamorized as the Noble Savage, representing a lost or vanishing human species deemed worthy of emulation or sustained nostalgia;
>
> seen as a harmless, childlike race in need of paternalistic guidance, self-improvement, education, civilization, conversion, and/or patronization;
>
> permanently consigned to an idealized past, frozen in history as an artifact who can be appreciated philosophically and aesthetically (as a "copper god" or a "natural philosopher") but who has no present political reality;
>
> seen as a good example to his/her people, having been converted and/or civilized by the dominant culture, of the ostensible benefits of such a conversion; and/or,
>
> considered to be a subservient yet honorable character, capable of assisting the dominant culture in the fulfillment of its destiny (the "my man Friday" syndrome).

Obviously, these conditions, like those that follow, have been interchanged and combined to produce characters of varying degrees of acceptability to the dominant culture.

Conditions of the "Negative" Stereotype
The "racial inferior":

> lacks a recognizable psychological reality, that is, has no motivation for his or her actions, emotional content, coherent thought processes and speech, personality, bodily self-awareness, cultural context, humor, or any "spiritual condition," or soul;

> *does* demonstrate any of the above in a negative and only negative connotation, that is, as "murderous," "rapacious," "primitive," "one-dimensional," "naked," "heathenish," "wooden," "full of gibberish," or "devilish";

> is portrayed as "less than human," animalistic, and lacking any conscious or moral motivation;

> has skin color or racial features that are exaggerated, caricatured, or in themselves taken as sufficient to deny him or her human status;

> has no historical or cultural reality, and thus must really be as portrayed by the defining entity, without recourse to self-defense, testimony, or other inalienable rights to an autonomous selfhood; and/or,

> is, by biblical definition or inference, a "child of the devil" and a hostile Other.

Examples of these criteria will be evident throughout this discussion in various manifestations. It should be emphasized that "negative" and "positive," or "good" and "bad" appellations regarding these stereotypes are entirely relative to the preconceptions and needs of the dominant culture, and that the use of any stereotype in the portrayal of Indians is considered here to be contributory to their dehumanization and deracination.

WHAT CONSTITUTES AN ARCHETYPE?

Self-naming and identity also emerge into consciousness, as Lippard and many psychologists suggest, from "inside" the individual, in the form of preconscious psychic experiences as a child; as dreams and "visions"; as the contents of subvocal speech; as intellectual deliberation; through identification with kin or friends, heroes, oral traditions, histories, rituals, myths, and cosmologies; and as the creative intelligence that empowers us to reinvent ourselves, employing a variety of quite subjective and intuitive phenomena. Within the epistemologies of religion and the "sciences" of genetics and psychology, many different models emerge that attempt to describe the subjective phenomena of self-generation and self-revelation, each using unique terminologies, many of which have come into common usage.

Some religions, for example, speak of the "inner voice" that contains the wisdom of the deity, sought through fasting, prayer, and meditation. Some Indian religions practice the shamanistic inducement of inner visions via the complex rituals of the "vision quest" and/or the ingestion of vision-inducing, psychotropic drugs such as datura (native tobacco), peyote, and mescaline. Since the discovery of the structure of the DNA molecule by Watson and Crick, a generation of geneticists have sought to explain how identity, both physical and psychical, might consist of a myriad of chemically programmed reactions that determine the way proteins interact to form unique, inborn, individual characteristics. Similarly, modern neuroscience is concerned with the production and interplay of "neurotransmitters" as they affect the psychic life generated in the brain. The tripartite psychological model of Sigmund Freud is widely known to consist of the subtle relationships between the ego, id, and superego that form and inform personality. These are just a few oversimplified examples of how identity constructed from "inside" the individual is thought to occur.

The word *archetype* has emerged into modern usage as part of a psychoanalytic model articulated principally by the Swiss psychologist C. G. Jung. It is, however, an ancient word first used, according to Jung, by Philo Judaeus, an early Greek philosopher, "with reference to the *Imago Dei* (God-image) in man." The word continued to be used by Gnostics, alchemists, and philosophers to denote a primal form or "material" (like "archetypal light" or "archetypal stone"), which they supposed to be the originary creative element of the universe.

In Jung's adaptation of the word, "we are dealing with archaic or—I would say—primordial types, that is, with universal images that have existed since the remotest times." Jung's concern with archetypes, like that of this discussion, is one of manifestation and transformation. His conception of the formation of individual and cultural identity, which he calls the "process of individuation," depends upon how the various archetypes emerge into consciousness: "The archetype is essentially an unconscious content that is altered by becoming conscious and by being perceived, and it takes its colour from the individual consciousness in which it happens to appear." What makes the Jungian concept of the archetypes useful in this discussion is their antithetical form and function in contrast to stereotypes, and the implication that, unlike stereotypes projected onto individuals from the outside, archetypes derive from within the individual via either the "personal unconscious" ("a more or less superficial layer") or the "collective unconscious" ("which does not derive from personal experience and is not a personal acquisition but is inborn"). Furthermore, Jung's own interest in the way in which "primitive tribal lore is concerned with archetypes that have been modified in a special way" will assist us in pursuing the intrinsic correlation between Indian histories and Indian identities, both ancient and modern.[3]

Archetypes, because they constellate in individual consciousnesses in different ways and are "coloured" by them, tend to produce heterogeneity and individualism, and may be seen as part of a dynamic model of identity formation. Stereotypes, on the other hand, tend to produce homogeneity and a static model of identity, fixed in language and in time. While both are ultimately concerned with images, "an experience *in images and of images*," the archetypes suggest a living, transitive, and thus historically active concept of identity, one involved in "making" the world.[4] When a race's history is erased, manipulated, or ignored, so then is its potential for a continued construction of identity. As mythologist Roland Barthes has suggested:

> The oppressed *makes* the world, he has only an active, transitive (political) language; the oppressor conserves [the world], his language is plenary, intransitive, gestural, theatrical: it is Myth. The language of the former aims at transforming, of the latter at eternalizing.[5]

Although Barthes tends to view all myth as stagnating, malignant, and oppressive, Jung perceives that there are, in practicality, two kinds of myth, one oppressive and the second liberating. In his discussion of archetypes, Jung makes a crucial distinction between those that have found expression in myth, fairy tale, and tribal lore, have "received a specific stamp and have been handed down through long periods of time," and have been codified as "tribal lore" or "the ruling world religions"; and those that emerge spontaneously as "complexes that come upon us like fate, [whose] effects are felt in our most personal life."[6] The first kind, like Christianity or the traditional cosmogenic myths of Indians, "all claim supreme authority for themselves" and are thus engaged in the cultural and religious warfare of the world. This type of myth "is constituted by the loss of the historical quality of things: in it things lose the memory that they were once made." Further, it "is a [type of] language which does not want to die: it wrests from the meanings which give it its sustenance an insidious, degraded survival, it provokes in them an artificial reprieve in which it settles comfortably, it turns them into speaking corpses."[7]

While myths in general first emerge, in any case, as fanciful, imaginative interpretations of the cosmos, the human panorama, and nature (usually in the form of legends, creation stories, folktales, poems, and the like), they may become static and acquire the stamp of dogma or a determinant theology. Ruth Underhill, a noted ethnographer of American Indians, has intimated how this profound change in the status of a myth can cause the deepest confusion and dissociation:

> Myth and ritual, which may be twins developed from the same ovum, can grow apart until the relationship is barely recognizable. To the thinker and seer, the belief was the religion and the ceremony simply its servant. To the Indian layman, the ceremony was the essential. From it he received security and courage, whereas the myth might be as vague as some fine points of theology are to the modern churchgoer.[8]

Myth, once separated from the imaginative and regenerative dramaturgy that was its human exercise, then becomes the province of the priesthood, the papacy, or the theologian, and as such loses much of its vitality and human usefulness.

The second class of myth, consisting of the "archetypes of transformation," resists supreme authority: "the one thing consistent with their nature is their *manifold meaning*, their almost limitless wealth of reference, which makes any unilateral formulation impossible."[9] In the discussion that follows, I have applied the first meaning of myth, or *mythos*, to denote the messianic, colonial imperative of Christianity that is based in a medium of high symbolism. The second I have reserved for those instances, in the literature and art that I discuss, that denote Indian characters, identities, and individuals that do not conform to the stamp of either their own codified religious tradition or of later colonial stereotypes. "They are ambiguous, full of half-glimpsed meanings," and, as such, represent authentic human beings engaged in "a rhythm of negative and positive, loss and gain, dark and light"—what has been called the "enantiodromia," or the vital play of opposites, in which each polarity is capable of transforming into its opposite, thus preventing stasis and entropy.[10]

But I hasten to emphasize that this distinction does not imply that all Indians are more inclined to individuation than to tradition, nor that all white Christians are more inclined to tradition than to individuation, but only that, over the course of American history, the significant trend has been to deprive Indians of their heterogeneous identities and histories so that white colonists might more easily advance their Christian agenda of imperial homogeneity. Indians are no more immune to the exercise of racial prejudice than are any of the other races of the world. Indeed, the focus of my interest is how codified myth of any origin can act as an adjunct to racial ideology, and how both collude in creating, in large part, the "hideous nightmare [that] lies upon the world."[11] Jung was alluding here to the more recent atrocities of German fascists in World War II, but the genocide of American Indians serves as yet another, more salient example, among many, of the colonial and postcolonial nightmare of ethnic genocide, now called more deflectively, "ethnic cleansing."[12]

AUTHORITY, AUTHORSHIP, AND AUTHENTICITY

Related to the structures of identity, history, and mythology, the issues of authority, authorship, and authenticity come into play as agents of power. If Indian history since 1492 has been "written" (authored) by white authority, then how can Indians attain or retain authentic identities in the present? The author of history also assumes the power of the author of identity and the arbiter of authenticity. Both "authority" and "authorship" derive from the Latin word *auctor*, meaning "originator," while "authentic" is defined as being "from an origin that cannot be questioned," giving rise to a triumvirate of linguistic power over identity. I would further offer this definition of "authenticity" as it might apply to Indian characters and images discussed in this book: Authenticity implies a conscious participation in the authorship of one's own identity, either collectively or individually.

Certainly no theoretical statement can accurately describe the multifaceted nature of feeling "authentic" within one's own personal cosmology or life situation. Those Indians who do not or cannot derive a feeling of authenticity from their racial identity, either because they are unenrolled or otherwise alienated from their tribal Indianness or because being Indian in and of itself is not a subjective point of identity, may always have other criteria for being authentic, or true to their own conception of identity. One can only suspect that, in the face of racial prejudice and historic oppression, the ability and desire to find one's authentic selfhood are severely affected by negative images of that self as a racial Other. Some analysts more postmodern than myself might even argue that there is no "authentic self," and indeed, as with identity, the terms and concepts are so slippery with metaphor that one is hard put to assert any viable definition of authenticity. Perhaps it is best to think of these things as the Hopi of Arizona think of their "Hopi-ness," that is, as something of a dialectical riddle: "True, honest, perfect words—that's what we call Hopi words. In all languages, not just in Hopi. We strive to be Hopi. We call ourselves Hopi because maybe one or two of us will become Hopi."[13] Such tangential logic ultimately prevails even in the most sophisticated models regarding the essentials of human identity, not because one wishes to obscure, but because one cannot be specific enough. I can speak of these things, as anyone can, only with regard to notions that seem appropriate to myself and my experiential vocabulary.

The origins of traditional Indian identities lie in the archaic past, and are contained in creation myths such as those of the Hopi, which I discuss in chapter 7. Significantly, the first words spoken by the "first people" in Hopi myth were: "Why are we here? Who are we?"—certainly questions concerned with identity. Like all autonomous cultures, the Hopi found their own unique answers to these questions. After the Conquest and the settlement of their land by whites, they and most other American Indian tribes were compelled to give up these answers, at least in part, to a new authority that denied their authenticity as a culture, and thus the authorship of that authenticity. For that reason, as Joanna Bigfeather says, "This is not acceptable." This is the premise with which I proceed, beginning with an analysis of the conception and perpetuation of stereotypes of the Indian, and followed by examples of what I believe to be significant deconstructions of those stereotypes and a concomitant construction (or recognition) of more archetypal figures by selected writers and artists, both Native and non-Native. What is at stake in the political and cultural realities that lie beyond and behind this mere analysis is of immense importance to the identities of not only American Indian and non-Indian peoples, but of a whole country and the future of its moral conscience and, indeed, its fruition as a truly "democratic" state. Until the majority of Americans have concurred, both formally and informally, that American Indians are equal and autonomous entities, entitled to every freedom and course of redress that pertains to its Christian majority, then that majority will have failed itself, its own religion, and its historical trajectory toward "freedom for all." Let us not deceive ourselves in assuming that modern Indians of the reservations and the urban diaspora are for the most part satisfied that the colonial past is over, or that white America has curbed its predatory and prejudicial ambitions. The stereotypes of the Indian still prevail, at least on many economic and political fronts, and still deprive them of their civil, treatied, and constitutional rights.

1

the language of conquest

necessity is the mother of reinvention   2

THE SEMIOLOGY AND PSYCHOLOGY OF CONQUEST

> We are the bold marauders,
> We are the white destroyers.
> And death will be our darling
> And Christ will be our name.
>
>   *Richard Fariña, "The Bold Marauder" (Vangaurd Records, 1971)*

The formulation and use of Indian stereotypes in American religious and political history goes back to the very beginnings of the colonial landfall on the North American continent, as is discussed more fully in chapter 3. More recently, the language of stereotype and scapegoating is easily discovered in the "official language" of the national leadership, in this case that of the Bureau of Indian Affairs (BIA), a federal agency founded on March 12, 1824. Between the years 1824 and 1977, forty-six men served as commissioners of the bureau, whose charge it was to formulate official policy regarding the "Indian problem" (indeed, to formulate the "Indian problem" itself) and to decide the fate of the three hundred thousand or so Indians remaining in the country preceding the last of the great "Indian Wars." Operating, at first and for a long while to come, under the manifestly paternal attitude that "Indians—like children—often did not know what was best for themselves," the commissioners of the BIA became both the spokesmen for the national conscience regarding the treatment of Indians and also the designers of a racial ideology with which to justify the westward expansion of Manifest Destiny, abetted in the 1820s and 1830s by John Marshall, first chief justice of the Supreme Court.[1] Their official proclamations and philosophical positions on the nature of the Indian reflect the prevailing notions of Indianness, and thus form a linguistic distillation in which we can sense the careful construction and perpetuation of Indian stereotypes.

With the notorious Indian fighter Andrew Jackson as president, the BIA's original position under Elbert Herring (1831–36) "exemplified the ethnocentrism that characterized Jacksonian Indian policy," a policy motivated by a racial ideology founded in and justified by Christian prejudice against anything non-Christian.[2] Jackson himself, according to David E. Stannard,

> had supervised the mutilation of 800 or so Creek Indian corpses— the bodies of men, women, and children that he and his men had massacred—cutting off their noses to count and preserve a record of the dead, slicing long strips of flesh from their bodies to tan and turn into bridle reins.[3]

Herring, writes Ronald Satz, "was unwilling to concede that the Indians might have a cultural distinctiveness and integrity worth preserving" and "found native civil laws, communal landholding patterns, non-Christian religious beliefs, and occupational preferences extremely obnoxious."[4] During his administration, the removal of most Indian tribes east of the Mississippi to "reservations" in the West commenced. Except for the Iroquois Nation of New York, some smaller tribes in upper New England, and some entrenched Seminoles who went into hiding in Florida, members of the Cherokee, Choctaw, Creek, Chickasaw, and Seminole tribes were removed some fifteen hundred miles along the now infamous Trail of Tears into the Territory of Oklahoma, under the Indian Removal Act of 1830. The bureau continued to operate on an either/or premise concerning the Indian: "The only alternatives left are, to civilize or exterminate them," announced Secretary of the Interior Alexander H. H. Stuart in 1852.[5] How best to "civilize" them became the ostensibly humanitarian mandate and the "white man's burden" of the bureau, and involved considerable consternation among its various commissioners, many of whom, having had no firsthand experience with Indians, were forced to rely on and amplify stereotypical notions of the Indian in order to justify their political maneuverings.

Federal Indian policy assumed several things about Indian culture that reinforced earlier stereotypes and created others. William Medill, commissioner from 1845 to 1849, assumed Indians to be "ignorant, degraded, lazy, and [in possession of] no worthwhile cultural traits." Medill possessed no prior knowledge of Indian affairs, yet was able to say, with great conviction, that too much federal support of impoverished tribal welfare led only to "the means of living for a time, independent of industry and exertion, in idleness and profligacy, until the indisposition to labor or the habit of intemperance becomes so strong, that [the Indian] degenerates into a wretched outcast."[6] He was a strong advocate of punishing inebriate Indians, whom he assumed to be legion, and was instrumental in introducing manual labor schools and religious missions onto the reservations. Medill's successor, Orlando Brown, professed in 1849 that by means of government policies of education and assimilation, "and with the aid of religious and benevolent societies, [Indians] may be, perhaps, turned from their roving habits, their thirst for war and bloodshed allayed, and they may be gradually won over to agriculture, and ultimately civilization."[7] The litany of obvious racism continued under Luke Lea (1850–53), who "believed the Indian to be a barbarian and often expressed horror over the actions of some of the 'wild' tribes."[8] Lea was eloquent in his justification for the "civilizing" of the Indian:

> When civilization and barbarism are brought in such relation that they cannot coexist together, it is right that the superiority of the former should be asserted and the latter compelled to give way. It is, therefore, no matter of regret or reproach that so large a portion of our territory has been wrested from its aboriginal inhabitants and made the happy abode of an enlightened and Christian people.[9]

Manifest Destiny has never had a more plainspoken advocate. Lea's administration was "troubled" by Apache skirmishes in the new Texas Territory, ceded to the United States by the Treaty of Guadelupe Hidalgo, by Indian resistance to the white onslaught in California prompted by the Gold Rush, and by the beginnings of the great Sioux Wars on the Plains.

By 1865, such sentiments as Lea's had achieved the level of national policy, and Dennis Nelson Cooley (1865–66) "clearly saw the elimination of Indian culture as a laudable objective."[10] During the previous year, Colonel John Chivington had perpetrated one of the two worst massacres in Indian history, the Sand Creek Massacre near Fort Lyon, Colorado, during which more than "200 Cheyennes were [slaughtered], more than half of them women and children," while a white flag of truce flew over their encampment.[11] Cooley referred to some of his Puebloan Indian wards as "the miserable lizard-eaters of Arizona," and was instrumental in making the "small-reservation system" a reality by gaining large treatied land cessions from the Osage, Choctaws, Chickasaws, and Cherokees, whose barely settled Oklahoma Territory was about to become a grab bag for white settlers during the Oklahoma Land Rush, under a new ruse called the Indian Allotment Act of 1887. One can imagine Cooley, after completing his "lizard-eaters" speech, retiring to Delmonico's in New York for a more sophisticated dinner of raw oysters, oxtail soup, and calf brains with scrambled eggs.

John Q. Smith (1875–77) again echoed the national consensus that the supposed nature of Indians, being composed chiefly of "ignorance, degradation, indolence, savagery, and superstition," was in itself cause for their oppression.[12] With Smith's administration, the beginning of the end of Indian military resistance to white colonization was realized during the War for the Black Hills (or Sitting Bull's and Crazy Horse's War, 1876–77), that was to culminate in 1890 with the Massacre at Wounded Knee. By 1883, a Court of Indian Offenses was inaugurated by Hiram Price "to abolish rights and customs so *injurious to Indians*," among which were "participation in certain dances, plural marriages, the destruction of property by mourners, the purchase of wives and concubines," and the engagement of medicine men in their "usual practices" (emphasis added).[13] It was hoped that such prohibitions, along with those introduced later against speaking Indian dialects, alcohol consumption, long hair, and tribal religious practices, would hasten the now brutalized "heathen" Indian along the road to Christian civilization. The goal, until the administration of John Collier in 1933, was consistent and unrelenting: "to impress American civilization upon the Indian, to whiten the red man," whether by political, religious, or military might.[14]

Recurring among the several viewpoints of commissioners are three central imperatives that are served by and demand a basic ignorance of Indian culture (a blissful ignorance, as it were) that made the cultural and possible physical genocide of Indians palatable to both the commissioners and the white population at large. First was the either/or, "us or them" position announced by Stuart in 1852 and echoed again in 1909 by Commissioner Robert Valentine: "It is possible to do only two things with the Indians," he said, "to exterminate them, or to make them into citizens. Whichever we choose *should be done in the most business-like manner*" (emphasis added).[15] It should be noted that in both instances, and throughout the history of the BIA, the word "extermination" does not refer to anything other than actual

Native American Indian (Sign of the Times), from the "Transitions, Inc." series, by Daniel Tisdale (graphite on photocopy, 1989). Although Tisdale's piece may seem far-fetched and satirical, the process of Christianizing, educating, civilizing, and otherwise "whitening" the Indian was intent on producing just such changes as Tisdale illustrates. (Courtesy of the artist.)

physical genocide; the implementation of cultural genocide falls on the other side of the coin, that of "civilization." Both options, then, constitute one form of genocide or another, a point that makes the supposed resolution of an "Indian question" rather moot.[16]

Second, as George M. Frederickson has pointed out, the first dilemma incorporates a subset of two related problems facing the Christian hegemony:

> There were two crucial distinctions which allowed Europeans of the Renaissance and Reformation period [and afterwards] to divide the human race into superior and inferior categories. One was between Christian and heathen and the other between "civil" and "savage."[17]

As the BIA went about its business trying to "civilize" its Indian wards, it consistently voiced its belief that civilization and Christianization were to go hand in hand toward helping the savage Indian achieve full membership in the human race. Commissioner Thomas Hartley Crawford (1838–45) was the first to recognize that the replacement of Indian traits with those of the white Christian might best be effected through a comprehensive reeducation effort: "Between 1838 and 1845, the commissioner drew on [his past] experience to help construct an educational system for Indians that was to have a profound impact on their lives and that survived for generations." Crawford also conjoined "civilization" with "Christianization" forever in the policies of the BIA: "Indians must be civilized, as well as, if not in order to their being, christianized."[18] Cooley later reinforced this alignment by encouraging the practice of "using religious denominations to oversee the transition from savagery to civilization."[19] This prospect was reaffirmed, during its actual continuance in practice from Crawford's day, by Roland E. Trowbridge who, in 1880, "retained the old rule that at each Indian agency a single [religious] denomination held an exclusive missionary franchise."[20] As late as 1923, the BIA reiterated its position that "it should do everything in its power to assist the religious volunteers who worked among the Indians." Although Charles Henry Burke (1921–29) was completely ignorant of Indian customs and ceremonials, he "instructed his superintendents to limit the duration of Indian dances and to put a halt to certain 'degrading ceremonials' which the missionaries charged were a part of the dances."[21] In his "Message to All Indians" of 24 February 1923, Burke wrote:

> I do not want to deprive you of decent amusement or occasional feast days, but you should not do evil or foolish things or take so much time for these occasions. No good comes from your "give-away" [potlatch] custom and dances, and it should be stopped. It is not right to torture your bodies or handle poisonous snakes in your ceremonies [as did the Hopi and other shamanistic societies]. All such extreme things are wrong and should be put aside and forgotten.[22]

Ruth Underhill, once a worker in the bureau, remembers the Hopi response to a similar exhortation made by a white official who, witnessing the "simulat[ed] sexual intercourse" of the Koshare or clown kachina dancers during a Soyal (winter solstice) ceremony, cried out, "Indecent! And with children present. We cannot tolerate this." "The Hopi priest," recalls Underhill,

> looked both amazed and sad. I do not remember how his answer was phrased by the interpreter but its import was, "How then do you wish us to teach our children about the beginnings of life? The man is a sacred messenger and his act is performed in a sacred place. How better could children understand that creating life is a sacred act? I have heard that, when white children talk about it, they laugh. Children in the kiva do not laugh."[23]

The bureau's policy, then, was one of depriving Indians of their sacred religious beliefs and practices while at the same time replacing them with Christian ones.

The historical effect of missionary work among American Indians is highly ambiguous. As with most things human, there were good and bad servants among both the BIA and the evangelical communities. While Indian communities were often met with censure, open hostility, and a pervasive greed, some were also welcomed into the missionizing project with friendly and compassionate contact. For a long while, missionaries, not governmental agencies, assumed responsibility for building hospitals and schools, supplying agricultural assistance and food, lobbying against white bootleggers and land-hungry despoilers, and generally caring for indigent and dispossessed Indians. And for a long while, these activities took place under the overt or implied necessity of converting Indians and dissolving their traditional religions and community ties.

A word of caution and actual governmental change in policy toward its missions (most of which were beholden to the government for their land and their military protection) finally surfaced in 1928, with the publication of the "Meriam Report," whose official name was "The Problem of Indian Administration." Its author, Lewis Meriam, a member of the board of directors of the Indian Rights Association, was called upon by Secretary of the Interior Hubert Work to direct a thorough social-science inquiry into the entire Indian problem. Writing in 1932 in *Facing the Future in Indian Missions,* Meriam directed his most cogent remarks to the missionary community, remarks that became increasingly influential in directing government policy under the BIA tenure of John Collier (1933–45). Reminding over-

Tom Toslino (Navajo) suffered more than an artistic makeover during his stay at the Carlisle Indian School in Pennsylvania beginning in 1882, where the motto was "Kill the Indian, Save the Man." (Photographs by John Choate, courtesy of the Denver Public Library.)

zealous missionaries that Indians "have a religion of their own which to them is satisfactory," and that some "may even be bitterly resentful of the activities of one who presumes to tell them he has a better religion," Meriam set forth several ideas (not the least of which was the constitutionality of religious freedom) that were to henceforth guide and control mission activities, particularly with regard to boarding schools, prohibition of Indian religious rites, and enforced conversion.[24] This moment in time pulled together a host of "friends of the Indian" who were to radically change the perception of Indianness in the minds of white America. (See chapter 5 for more on the Collier administration.)

Third among the bureau's most overriding imperatives was to act in the "best interests" of its Indian wards with regard to the allocation and management of Indian lands. Implied in this "burden," of course, was the stereotypical and expedient notion that Indians were not competent to rule over their own lands (those few million acres that were indeed left for them to manage). Also at stake was the question of whether Indians had lawful claim to any of the lands they had occupied before contact and colonization, despite over four hundred treaties to the contrary. By the 1860s, "Congress and the public had begun to doubt that Indian tribes had any valid aboriginal land claims."[25]

The administration of Cato Sells (1913–21) perhaps best exemplifies how the ostensibly good intentions of the bureau regarding Indian land were, and are, irreconcilably intertwined with colonial imperialism. Caught in the middle between land-hungry whites and "incompetent" Indians whose land allotments had run out of federal protection twenty-five years after the Dawes (or Indian Allotment) Act of 1887, Sells tried his best to defend Indians against both taxation and other means of usurpation of their land parcels. The BIA heretofore had allotted some 138 million acres of reservation land to individual Indian families, in the hopes that private ownership would break down tribal relations and thus accelerate the assimilation of Indians into the greater capitalist society of private landholders and entrepreneurs. The ostensible "good intentions," as proffered by John D. C. Atkins (1885–88), promised "Indian progress and development" toward an agrarian economy, "self-sufficiency, personal independence, and material thrift."[26] As usual, it was not admitted (but well-known among BIA bureaucrats) that most Indians preferred holding their land in common, either as clans or tribes, and had not the faintest desire to own land privately.

The dramatic diminishment of Indian lands between 1500 and the present was but one of the impoverishing effects of Bureau of Indian Affairs policy. (Reprinted with permission from *Since Predator Came: Notes from the Struggle for American Indian Liberation*, Ward Churchill [Littleton, Colorado: Aigis Publications, 1995]. Map by Alexandria Lord.)

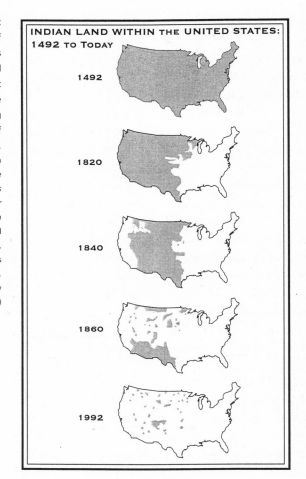

INDIAN LAND WITHIN THE UNITED STATES: 1492 TO TODAY

1492

1820

1840

1860

1992

Twenty-five years later, when the federal trust protecting these allotments ran out, Sells found that most Indians still remained or had been declared "incompetent" (by BIA criteria) to assume fee simple ownership of their allotments, which meant in effect that the allotments remained under the control of the BIA, as did the fates of the Indian tribes who held them. Many of those who were deemed "competent," half of whom were among the reservation Indians of Oklahoma, quickly sold their land to white entrepreneurs. It became common practice during the period following allotment for white and Hispanic profiteers to delude newly landed Indians into the sale or long-term lease of their land parcels.

Ironically, while the bureau failed to break down tribal affiliations as intended by the Dawes Act, it also failed to force Indians into assimilation and enculturation; by the 1990s the reservation system is still the norm, and "incompetent" Indians still largely the wards of the BIA. Between 1887 and 1934, as a result of the failure of the Dawes Act, traditionally Indian lands were reduced by some 60 percent through broken treaties, white purchases, leases, and government reallocation. To this day, the management of most remaining Indian lands in the contiguous forty-eight states is assumed by the BIA and the Department of the Interior, whose propensity it is to provide white businessmen (mining companies, ranchers, water grantees, oil drillers, lumber companies, etc.) with lucrative leases on Indian land.

BIA land policy following allotment was largely based on the stereotype of incompetent, indolent Indians, despite their generally responsible history of environmental stewardship through centuries of hunting, gathering, and subsistence farming. The BIA leadership wanted Indians to become large-scale farmers, ranchers, and entrepreneurs but at the same time offered them reservations on the least productive land for such enterprises, often arid or semiarid land seemingly devoid of any productive potential. Typical of the confused and generally obstructionist thinking that accompanied BIA land policy, local bureau offices were put in charge of managing allotments and subsequent profits from what turned out to be vast reserves of oil, timber, coal, natural gas, copper, and other valuable resources discovered later on the reservations. This provincialism encouraged widespread graft and corruption with regard to Indian accounts supervised by government officials, a legacy that continues into the late 1990s. In 1996, for instance, the Native American Rights Fund filed suit against the secretary of the interior, the assistant secretary for Indian affairs, and the secretary of the treasury, alleging gross mismanagement of over $2.5 billion in Indian accounts over the previous twenty years; audits will go back even further. Most, if not all, of this money was collected on behalf of Indians for land and resource leases on reservations; it has since "disappeared."[27]

Although most modern tribes have their own governing structures and legal systems, the BIA and Department of Interior often control land usage and mineral rights, and thus determine the economic viability of Indian communities. The stereotype of the incompetent Indian, as we will see, has been taken up by such authors as Oliver La Farge, Frank Waters, and Linda Hogan, and the policies of the BIA, whose real "literary" function was to "write" the Indian stereotype for the public imagination, are accurately ridiculed by modern Indian artists such as Jaune Quick-to-See Smith and Jesse Cooday.

Whatever humanitarian feelings toward the Indian some commissioners might have held (and, to be fair, some did harbor and express genuine custodial instincts and compassion, and John Collier was a true advocate for Indian rights and sovereignty), the cumulative effect of 170 years of BIA policymaking has been to amplify popular stereotypes of Indians in order to wrest from them their Indianness, whether that be exemplified by their religion, land, livelihood, culture, or, ultimately, their lives.

MEET YOUR MAKER: A SEMIOLOGICAL VIEW

That the mythos of Christianity has played such an important role in the process of deracinating and marginalizing Indians should not go unnoticed; it is indeed part and parcel of the "whiteness" that Indians have been forced to emulate upon threat of their extermination. Certainly it can be said, after examining the "national language" of the federal bureaucracy, that the conceptualization of the Indian as an alien and hostile Other, even as the devil incarnate, is largely derived from the sacrosanct, mythological language of certain sects of Christianity. Indeed, the commissioners of the BIA depended on Christian missionary zeal and the great converting imperatives of its mythos for just that purpose: to dehumanize the Indian Others in order to justify their extinction, or at least their acquiescence, as significant or signifying human entities.

This process of stereotyping the Other via a mythic imperative has been well analyzed by such eminent "mythologists" as Roland Barthes and Jean Baudrillard, both of whom are also concerned with the phenomena of colonization and enculturation. Essential to understanding how and why stereotypes are born is an understanding of the motivation of the stereotyping agency, in this case that of the westering American Christian. "Myth has an imperative, buttonholing character," argues Barthes, "stemming from an historical concept [like Manifest Destiny], directly springing from contingency [like the removal of the Indian from the path of Christian progress]."[28]

Religious myths always have a certain encoded power that derives from their supposedly divine origins, a power that can be exercised against, rather than for, the benefit of humanity. Despite the likelihood that Christ, being a Palestinian Jew, was probably not a white man at all, European Christians generally imagined him to be, and, in the context of their participation in the colonization of the "dark races," frequently assumed that people of any ethnicity not carrying the genes of "whiteness" were thus heathenish, or less than human, and certainly were not children of the great white God of Albion or Seville. Ethnic or racial inferiority, then, became part of the larger framework wherein conquered or about-to-be-conquered indigenous peoples could be seen by the colonizer as nonhumans who could be, and were, treated with the utmost cruelty. Because they have been stereotyped as "uncivilized heathen" in need of an inoculation of "whiteness," the Indians of the Western Hemisphere have suffered not only the denigration of their own tribal religions, but also the brutalization of being stereotyped as less-than-human entities, unworthy of basic human decency. The BIA policy of "whitening the red man" can thus be seen as a universal policy employed by the mythos of Christianity in all colonial episodes involving racially or religiously antithetical parties.

Barthes has the following to say about the process of inoculation as it affects the "red man":

> ideology continuously transforms the products of history into essential [stereo]types. . . . it cannot rest until it has obscured the ceaseless making of the world, fixated this world into an object which can be forever possessed, catalogued its riches, embalmed it, and injected into reality some purifying essence which will stop its transformation, its flight towards other forms of existence.[29]

Indians, given the BIA options of extermination or civilization, have of course generally resisted both with all of their "transitive" will, because they have perceived that there really is no option at all. Indeed, they have tried to "flee," to preserve their forms of existence, but were encapsulated on reservations and forced into compliant enculturation.

Indians today, more articulate than ever in realizing the precariousness of their situation, understand the necessity of finding an antidote to inoculation and deracination. Echoing Barthes, who surmises that "the best weapon against myth is perhaps to mythify it in its turn," Salt River Pima Earl Ray says: "Our Indian kids today are going to find life twice as challenging as the non-Indian. They have to learn to take both ways and interweave them—

taking things where they apply—take mythology and use it as a political tool."[30] A similar notion is expressed by Underhill, an early observer of Indian ceremonials, when she wishes that such powerful rituals as the Navajo Night Chant might "somehow be carried over to the problems of modern Navaho life! If some genius of 'the People' could change the theme of chants and sand paintings so that they might supply power for the new problems, how many negative attitudes would shift to positive."[31] We will see how this same strategy applies in the literary and artistic works of La Farge, Waters, Simon Ortiz, Linda Hogan, Quick-to-See Smith, and Diego Romero, all of whom effectively "appropriate" or incorporate Indian legends and iconography as a countermyth to the racist ideologies of Euramerica. Their various retellings and articulations of Indian cosmogenic stories, of Indian cultural practices, and of traditional symbolism invoke the primordial power of Indianness as a humanizing and equalizing force in their art.

It seems apparent from the BIA files that some of the most effective and powerful among its commissioners were precisely those who had little or no knowledge of Indians or Indian culture. Those who spoke most convincingly about the "degrading" nature of Indian religion had never witnessed a ceremonial; those who were most enthusiastic about reeducation and assimilation had never visited a pueblo or heard an Abenaki creation myth; those who were most involved with relocation and the reservation system, and the presumptuous notion that agriculture or cattle raising was the best life for Indians, had no knowledge of their traditional lifeways as nomadic or hunter-gatherer peoples; and those most revolted by their supposed savagery and barbarity had never met a real Indian. As writer and Indianist Oliver La Farge commented, in a 1940 review of Commissioner Burke's "Message to All Indians": "These were the only friends the Indians had, these people who could not see the beauty of a Tewa Eagle Dance, were deaf to the clear music of a Kiowa singer, unable to imagine good in the wild majesty of the Navajo Fire Ceremony."[32]

All of these instances, at first, seem ironic, or at least to reflect a dismal incompetence among the majority of the commissioners. But, in practice, their very distance from their work facilitated the purpose of their office, which was to perpetuate extant stereotypes of the Indian and to create new ones when the need arose. To know Indians too well, or even at all, would have been a hindrance in their conceptualization and "simulation" of the Indian in the cause of colonial expansion. This separation, this intentional and blissful ignorance, brings us to another aspect of the birth and propagation of stereotypes: the process of "simulation" as expressed by Jean Baudrillard.

Both stereotypes and archetypes are concerned with images, as is the "precession of simulacra" that engages Baudrillard. As Baudrillard understands it, the further from a "basic reality" an image is, the more it tends to be a total abstraction, or "simulation." Baudrillard outlines this precession as follows:

> This would be the successive phases of the image:
>
> it is the reflection of a basic reality
>
> it masks and perverts a basic reality
>
> it masks the absence of a basic reality
>
> it bears no relation to any reality whatever: it is its own simulacrum.[33]

We can safely assert here that the first phase of the image comprises, for our purposes, completely "real" and fully human Indians, existing as a physical and psychological reality in a particularized extant culture. They are Indians as they know themselves to be, situated in history and in place, living day-to-day lives pertaining to their own needs—creating, destroying, eating, thinking, copulating, etc. Baudrillard hypothesizes that this first order is "of the order of sacrament"; that it is "good" in that it is so essential as to be pure existence.[34] Now for BIA bureaucrats to acknowledge that such "real" Indians existed would indeed have defeated their whole purpose and caused them no end of self-scrutiny and self-consciousness. It would certainly have aborted their mission by rendering the "heathen" as autonomous human entities sacrosanct in their own reality. It would, in Baudrillard's words, have dissuaded them from their Christian mandate, from their "delirious illusion of uniting the world under the aegis of a single principle." Instead, as we have noted, the BIA and other image makers of the nineteenth and early twentieth centuries have successfully opted for, and in large part created, the second stage of the image, "an evil appearance—of the order of malefice": stereotyped Indians as we have seen them portrayed above.[35] "Thus, at the beginning of colonization," continues Baudrillard,

> there was a moment of stupor and amazement before the very possibility of escaping the universal law of the Gospel. There

were two possible responses: either to admit that this law was not universal, or to exterminate the Indians so as to remove the evidence.[36]

Luckily for the BIA, Christian missionaries had evolved a third possibility, that of "mental colonization," as Frantz Fanon has called it, or of conversion and civilization, an aesthetic compromise that would not make the bureau appear as barbaric as the Indians were alleged to be, and would not, in effect, be any less deadly to real Indians. The simulated Indian, "an evil appearance," would naturally lead to his own demise in the face of white goodness and righteousness.

The construction of the Other also involves psychological and semiological processes driven by the grey eminence of politics and the inability of the "master race" to admit that any race other than its own can possibly be essentially viable or real. As Edward Said has noted, based on his own Middle Eastern colonial experiences, "In this view, the outlying regions of the world have no life, no history, or culture to speak of, no independence or integrity worth representing without the West."[37] Herein we can understand why the American media have long insisted on portraying all Indians as being alike. Raymond William Stedman, writing about the persistence of clichés and stereotypes of the Indian in modern film, literature, television, and advertising, notes that "all Indians have one national, ethnic, and linguistic identity . . . all Indians look, think, and talk alike."[38] Similarly, we find in American movies generic Indian characters who, until recently, have reflected no tribal idiosyncracies or personalities. The simulated Indian of Hollywood thus achieves the desired homogeneity that belies the immense diversity and heterogeneity of actual Indian nations, tribes, clans, and individuals, in order that myth might prevail. Commissioner William A. Jones (1897–1904) unconsciously promoted the utility of such a sameness in prodding the Other to become assimilated into the larger homogeneity of white culture, and thus to disappear: "As a self-supporting, useful member of society," Jones prophesied, "the Indian will pass out of our national life as a painted, feather-crowned hero [a stereotype of the Plains Indian] . . . to add the current of his free, original American blood to the heart of this great nation."[39] When Indians, as a homogeneous fictional entity, can then be consigned to the larger fiction of a mythology of the Other, they are voided of historical truth, cultural diversity, and any archetypal relationship with the "real world," and become stereotypes to be manipulated by their oppressors into a nonexistence preliminary to their ultimate extirpation.

PURITAN PROJECTION: A PSYCHOLOGICAL VIEW

As we know from history, many Others besides the Indian have suffered the consequences of Euramerican colonial thinking. In fact, the only racial/ethnic group not to have been consigned to Otherness in America is that of the white Anglo-Saxon Protestant (WASP) male of either English or Dutch/German descent. Irish Catholics, Chinese, Japanese, Vietnamese, Polish, Italians, Arabs, Jews, Hispanics, Russians, and various other racial/ethnic groups, as well as women and homosexuals, have all endured the marginalizing prejudices of the WASP mentality throughout the course of American history. Although such prejudicial thinking is not unique to America, or even to WASPs in general, the particular psychological and semiological dynamics involved in formulating Otherness in America seem curiously attached to the psychology of Protestant Christendom, especially in the forms of Calvinist Puritanism and Lutheran Protestantism. These are, of course, the worldviews of the religious founders of the United States, the "master race" in America. Catholicism served the same purpose in much of Europe, Asia, South America, Mexico, and Canada: Catholics were there first. As Frantz Fanon argues, "All forms of exploitation resemble one another. They all seek the source of their necessity in some edict of a biblical nature."[40] Fanon represents the Others of the black races of Africa and the West Indies and, as a psychologist and intellectual also schooled in French imperialism, helps articulate the psychological aspects of colonial myth making.

Relying heavily on the Jungian concepts of "projection" and "the shadow," Fanon offers up a cohesive paradigm for the mental formulation of the Other that may in fact precede the linguistic manifestation. "The scapegoat for white society, which is based on myths of progress, civilization, liberalism, education, enlightenment, refinement," he postulates, "will be precisely the force that opposes the expansion and triumph of these myths," which, in the case at hand, are Native Americans defending their country and culture. The Jungian concept of projection involves those psychological mechanisms by which the Indian becomes the "red devil," an antithesis of the white man's image of himself that, paradoxically, emerges from within himself.

As Fanon succinctly puts it, "This mechanism of projection [works thusly]: In the degree to which I find in myself something reprehensible, only one solution remains for me: to get rid of it, to ascribe its origin to someone else." In so doing, one "authors" that "someone else." One can see this process written into the (white) history of Indians: they, not we, are the bloodthirsty savages; they, not we, are the rapacious land-hungry manipulators; theirs, not ours, is the primitive, superstitious religion; they, not we, are the incarnation of evil; and so on. For black people, the intrinsic whiteness of Christian goodness made them a de facto symbol of all that was dark, unconscious, and uncivilized: "Those Negroes were the principle of evil."[41] This dynamic plays out the same way with Indians (the "red devils") or the Chinese/Japanese (the "yellow peril"), "the thieving Jew," and so on ad infinitum. The overwhelming frequency of Other making among the Puritan forefathers, those most repressed and repressive of all Christians, suddenly seems to make sense in light of the theory of projection; they, as Nathaniel Hawthorne knew only too well, were themselves possessed of a savagely "persecuting spirit," "being of the most intolerant brood that ever lived."[42]

The early Puritans conceived themselves to be intimately involved in a transhistorical drama in which the ultimate intentions and apocalyptic judgments of their Lord and Creator were to be acted out on Earth. As a result, their contacts with Indians in the New Zion they hoped to create in America were fraught with symbolic associations of a biblical nature. Both good and bad versions of the Indian appear frequently in Puritan letters and sermons, their contrasting valuations due largely to the way Indians deported themselves with regard to the Puritan agenda. Incidents of hostility from the Indians of Powhatan caused Puritans the utmost fear, by which they projected onto the Indian various negative images. The preacher Cotton Mather was especially virulent in his assessment of the Indians as the scourge of God, as was his father, Increase, both of whom enlarged on the captivity tale of Mary Rowlandson (published in 1682), who described her captors as "aetheistical, proud, wild, cruel, barbarous, brutish, (in one word) diabolical Creatures. . . . the worst of heathen."[43] Robert Berkhofer, citing the work of Michael Rogin and others, echoes Fanon's argument for projection in saying: "If the Puritans, for example, could project their own sins upon people they called savages, then the extermination of the Indian became a cleansing of those sins from their own midst as well as the destruction of a feared enemy."[44] If Indians brought food to their table or helped them clear land for planting, on the other hand, they were seen as "good Indians" acting out the providential nature of the Puritan God. The concept of projection as a form of psychological witchcraft is further taken up in chapter 7, in connection with the experiences of Frank Waters among the Hopi.

BIA policy, perceived as literature of the most banal yet representative sort, offers an introduction to the mass-produced imagistic canon of the Indian as a topic for general literary and artistic treatment. Indeed, the Indian was an almost ubiquitous character in "pioneer" literature and art, most of which made the notions of the BIA and its Puritan progenitors into stock characters who have, with few exceptions, retained their stereotypical dimensionlessness unto the present day. While I will not attempt to canvass the entire catalogue of Indian images that have emerged into the popular imagination over the last five centuries, a task that has already been carried out most effectively by such writers as Stedman and Berkhofer, I will enunciate some of the major stereotypes, in order to show how the writers and artists whose work I will discuss have made significant, perhaps revolutionary, alterations and expansions in the service of debunking these stereotypes. Some, like La Farge, Waters, Walter Ufer, and Helen Hunt Jackson, have done so largely to help save the Indian from both physical and cultural extinction, a motive as political as that which drives the BIA and as semiologically and psychologically mythic in nature as the Christian metalanguage of Otherness, emerging in their literature and art as characters of fiction. Others, mostly modern Indian writers and artists, do so to articulate their Indianness, to write their own identities, and to focus the world's attention on their ongoing struggle for political and intellectual sovereignty.

wroughten scoundrels 3

The Noble Savage image is as much a stereotype as the ignoble one.
Robert F. Berkhofer Jr.

Even from their first crucial encounters with Native Americans, the white Pilgrims, like the Spanish conquistadors before them, began to manufacture the Other around them to avoid having to admit that these might be real human beings with sacramental natures of their own. They were of course preconditioned by the existing literature on Indians in France, Spain, and England as to what to expect from Native Americans. Columbus was the first commentator to attach a dualistic, good Indian/bad Indian character to the Natives. While his Caribs were cannibals, so his Arawak tribesmen were "timorous," generous to a fault, and religious. Francisco de Coronado, riding up from New Spain after the Mexican Conquest had decimated the Aztecs and subdued the other indigenous tribes of Mexico, was prepared to tolerate Indians as long as they were forthcoming as to the whereabouts of gold and silver in what is now the American Southwest. Seeking the fabled Seven Cities of Cibola, alluded to by the Spanish explorer-turned-mystic, Cabeza de Vaca, Coronado found the Puebloan and Apache Indians of Arizona and New Mexico to be accommodating if they were routinely threatened with military force. Coronado's scribe noted the "intelligence" these tribes showed in not trusting much that the invaders said or did: "They did not trust those who did not keep their word."[1] He also noted that the Hopi, in particular, as well as the other Puebloan tribes, always "came peacefully [at first], saying that they had come to offer the whole province and they wanted [Coronado] to be friends with them and to accept the presents which they gave him."[2] As noted in the previous chapter, the Puritans in their turn also had ambivalent notions of the Indian, and the principal enduring stereotypes of the Rousseauian Noble Savage and the colonial Ignoble Savage found new life in the Puritan literature of the 1600s. Within these two major types, a number of subtypes appear in various contexts.

Diaries and letters of the early colonists, sermons and religious proclamations, and published literature such as travel accounts, pamphlets, and captivity tales brim with descriptions of the Indian in different lights. A pamphlet by Alexander Whitaker contains a consistent example of the Indian as "red devil" that deserves repeating here:

> Let the miserable condition of these naked savages of the devil move you to compassion towards them. They acknowledge that there is a great God, but they know him not, wherefore they serve the devil for fear, after a most base manner. . . . They live naked of body, as if the shame of their sin deserved no covering. . . . They esteem it a virtue to lie, deceive, steal . . . if this be their life, what think you shall become of them after death, but to be partakers with the devil and his angels in hell for evermore?[3]

Added to this account were further descriptions of the predatory, brutish, warlike, bloodthirsty Indian who dashed children's brains out against tree trunks, raped and scalped white colonists, tortured captives (in an imaginative variety of ways), and burned and pillaged white settlements from Connecticut to Oregon. Later embellishments on this negative stereotype were the "reservation Indian," indolent, usually drunk, and generally incompetent; the "Mission Indian," squalid, pathetic, and cowardly; the "statesman Indian," crafty, deceitful, and treacherous; and the "stupid Indian," full of gibberish, irascible, and childlike. Any or all of these attributes could be combined arbitrarily by the white writer or artist into innumerable other concoctions of the "bad" Indian who became the stuff of fiction, poetry, political propaganda, anthropological monographs, theater, cinema, and the pictorial arts. Many such types persist even unto the present day.

Such late-nineteenth-century descriptions of Indians as the following, startling one by Mark Twain in *Roughing It* (1872), attest to the historical persistence of negative racial stereotyping. Twain's description distills into one paragraph many of the commonly perceived stereotypes of his day. He is describing the Gosiute Indians of the Great Basin:

> Such of the Goshoots as we saw, along the road and hanging about the stations, were small, lean, scrawny creatures; in complexion a dull black like the ordinary American negro; their faces and hands bearing dirt which they had been hoarding and accumulating for months, years, and even generations, according to the age of the proprietor; a silent, sneaking, treacherous-looking race; taking note of everything, covertly, like all the other "Noble Red Men" that we (do not) read about, and betraying no sign in their countenances; indolent, everlastingly patient and tireless, like all other Indians; prideless beggars—for if the beggar instinct were left out of the Indian he would not "go," any more than a clock without pendulum; hungry, always hungry, and yet never refusing anything that a hog would decline; hunters, but having no higher ambition than to kill and eat jackass rabbits, crickets, and grasshoppers, and embezzle carrion from the buzzards and coyotes; savages who, when asked if they have the common Indian belief in a Great Spirit, show something which almost amounts to emotion, thinking whiskey is referred to; a thin scattering race of almost naked black children, these Goshoots are, who produce nothing at all, and have no villages, and no gatherings together into strictly defined tribal communities—a people whose only shelter is a rag cast on a bush to keep off a portion of the snow, and yet who inhabit one of the most rocky, wintry, repulsive wastes that our country or any other exhibit.[4]

What Twain notices herein, of course, is but the pitiful state in which rampant white colonialism had left the once-thriving Great Basin Indians who, although they practiced no agriculture because of their harsh environs, eked out a meager existence hunting and gathering. Once part of the assortment of tribes who inhabited this extreme environment—the Paiute, Ute, Shoshone, and Bannock—the Gosiutes have few progeny in the present.

The history of the Indian in American film provides a fairly consistent glossary of typical "bad Indian" motifs even up into the 1990s. Perhaps no Hollywood star exemplifies the movie industry's approach to Indians as succinctly as John Wayne, whose many roles as an Indian-hater and stalwart champion of American imperialism as both cowboy and pioneer endeared him to aficionados of the western genre movie. Before Wayne, a tradition had evolved in Hollywood of rescue films that, like the captivity tale of Mary Rowlandson, capitalized on the image of the brute, rapacious Indian who lays his devilish hands on a hapless white heroine. In his chapter entitled "And You Know What They Do to White Women," Raymond Stedman details the procession of this genre from the 1903 one-reeler *Rescue of Child from Indians* through D. W. Griffith's *The Battle at Elderbush Gulch* (1913), *The Last of the Mohicans* (1936), and *Northwest Passage* (1940) to John Ford's highly acclaimed vehicle for Wayne, *The Searchers*, produced in 1956.[5] Ironically, this last film was originally acclaimed not only for its complex screenplay (by Frank Nugent, derived from an Alan LeMay novel) but for its "antiracist" sentiment regarding Indians. I say "ironically," because the film itself is hardly antiracist as we would interpret that evaluation today.

In *The Searchers*, Wayne is cast as Ethan Edwards, a returning Confederate soldier who comes home to his brother's family in what is ostensibly Texas (though the film was shot in the Technicolor country of Monument Valley). The Indians portrayed herein are Comanches (or "Comanch," as Wayne pronounces it), and are depicted as a roving band of murdering, pillaging, and raping savages. Moments into the story, these Indians raid the pioneer homestead while Wayne, Martin (the half-breed adopted son of Wayne's brother, played by Jeffrey Hunter), and Ward Bond, as a clergyman and Texas Ranger, are lured away by the Comanches. Wayne's brother and his wife are killed (and she presumably raped), while his two nieces, Lucy and Debby, are abducted by the Indians. Wayne and Martin, whom Wayne barely tolerates because of his mixed blood, proceed on a prolonged five-year search for the missing girls, during which we witness Wayne the Indian-hater at his virulent worst.

Several events, both linguistic and physical, accentuate the racism evoked in the film. First, Wayne's attitude toward Indians shows a generalized racism that is projected through his dialogue. There is perpetual usage of the terms "buck," "Injun," and "squaw" (artist Jaune Quick-to-See Smith has remarked, half-jokingly, that the word "squaw" refers to the fact that Indian women "squawked when we were raped"). After the search party finds niece Lucy dead (raped and presumably mutilated, since they don't recover her body), Wayne remarks: "They'll keep her [Debby] until she comes of age to . . . well, you know." Coming upon some other captured white women now in the custody of the U.S. Cavalry, all of whom are crazed beyond reason by their experiences among the Indians, an officer remarks, "It's hard to believe they're white," to which Wayne replies, "They ain't white no more. They're Comanch." When they finally find an older Debby (played by Natalie Wood), Wayne comments to Chief Scar, her captor, that "you speak pretty good English for a Comanch." Debby, since her capture, has evidently become a wife of Chief Scar and doesn't wish to return to the white world, saying that "these are my people now." This revelation, combined with the nuance that Debby has had carnal knowledge with an Indian, enrages Wayne so much that he wishes to kill her. After he is wounded in a skirmish with Chief Scar's tribe, and presumably near death, Wayne acknowledges that Scar's Indianness has contaminated even Debby's blood. Bequeathing his earthly belongings to Martin, who protests, saying "Debby's your blood kin," Wayne pronounces, "Not anymore . . . She's been living with a buck." Though Wayne has a change of heart at the end, all this pernicious dialogue has served to illustrate the intense hatred Wayne's character has for Indians simply because they are of another, alien race. And though he forgives Debby, he murders and scalps Chief Scar. The issue of Debby's blood being tainted by her sexual encounter with an Indian is the main theme of the film, and emphasizes the sexualization of racism and the lingering insinuations of eugenics that I discuss more fully in chapter 4.

Other, physical events in the movie further denigrate the images of the Indian characters. Upon finding a dead Indian buried beneath some rocks, Wayne shoots out the dead man's eyes to deny him an afterlife. A later scene involves Martin unwittingly trading cheap hats for an Indian wife, who, despite Martin's protestations, slavishly follows him on foot to his campsite. When she tries to lie down at his side at bedtime, Martin cruelly kicks her down a hill, to the approving laughter of Wayne. The issue of the Indian as chattel, as slave and pariah, is embarrassingly plain here. "Regrettably," notes Stedman, "because he is John Wayne, because he is so untiringly skillful in the pursuit, his motivation dominates in building audience attitude."[6] " 'Livin' among the Comanches ain't livin' " is the final verdict that falls on

Indian life in this sorry film, whose creation in 1956 projects Puritan and proto-western stereotypes well into the modern age.

Also regrettably, Wayne's character offscreen was not much more enlightened toward Indians. Jesse Cooday, a Tlingit artist, has created a telling image entitled *Wayne's World 1992* that consists of a simple line drawing of Wayne in cowboy regalia, overprinted in orange and blue with the image of a Tlingit ceremonial mask, as if to "deface" Wayne's image and supplant it with an Indian one. Beneath the image is printed graphic text uttered at some point by Wayne in real life: "I don't feel we did wrong in taking this great country from them. There were great numbers of people who needed new land and the Indians were selfishly trying to keep it all for themselves."[7]

The cinematic and offscreen influence that such great American idols as Wayne could wield against the Indian character was of course abetted by the monied interests behind them. Since no Indians have yet had the financial wherewithal to produce a major motion picture on their own behalf, the genre has naturally been controlled by wealthy non-Indians, who have had little interest in real Indians beyond their potential for self-subverting roles in hackneyed plots where they "bite the dust" of their white leads. For an exhaustive accounting of negative Indian stereotypes in film, see Stedman's 1982 work, *Shadows of the Indian.*

GOOD INDIANS CAN BE BOUGHT HERE

While one is sometimes tempted to consider that good images of the Indian as Noble Savage, "nobleman of the forest," or "Roman of the plains," are acceptable even as stereotypes because they offset their negative counterparts and promote a white tolerance, even adulation, of Indianness, this position is not wisely taken, for it too deprives Indians of a historical reality apart from white projections. The development of the Noble Savage ideal is well known to be principally the work of French intellectuals of the Enlightenment and Romantic periods (Rousseau, Voltaire, Chateaubriand, and Diderot, especially), who embellished earlier colonial accounts of the Indian for their own philosophical ends. Perhaps the principal works influencing these Frenchmen were those of the French expatriate Baron de Lahontan, who published his *Dialogues avec un sauvage* in 1703, and the writings called *Relations,* published yearly by Jesuits in Quebec from 1632 to 1674. Both put forth a comprehensive and enticing image of the American Native as a Greeklike embodiment of nobility, bodily perfection, keen intelligence, subtle feeling, valor, prudence, and high moral character—all derived from an instinctual and innocent relationship with nature and the Great Spirit.

"It is important to know," remarks Georges Sioui of *Dialogues avec un sauvage,* "that Lahontan's observations date from the most troubled period in the development of New France, a time when other observers created the negative image of the Amerindian that still does so much harm."[8] While Sioui is defensive of Lahontan's "dialogues" with his adopted Huron brother, Adario, who enunciates the ostensibly "real" qualities of Indian religion, laws, medicine and health, and social customs, and while the authenticity of Lahontan's and Adario's description of Huron life has not been disputed successfully, in the context of myth making such descriptions have become universalized and hackneyed as part of a white-constructed image of little but romantic substance. Berkhofer tellingly observes that

> in this way the American Indian became part of the *bon sauvage* or Noble Savage tradition so long an accompaniment of the Golden Age or paradisical mythology of Western civilization. First the natives discovered and conquered by the Spanish and then those invaded by the French and English joined the *bon éthiopien, bon oriental,* and *bon nègre* as a convention for enunciating the hopes and desires of European authors.[9]

Furthermore, the image of the Noble Savage is, like that of the Ignoble Savage, based purely on the moral and ethical foundations of Anglo, European, and Euramerican cultures and, as a romantic construct, portrays the Indian as outside of history and in the realm of mythology, making it easy for whites to project this image, along with that of Christian goodness, onto the Indian as a sign of complicity in the saga of colonization.

One way to imagine the danger of images like the Noble Savage is to notice their purposeful exoticism. The Noble Savage is often pictured as a stoic red man replete with ceremonial (usually Plains Indian) headdress, breechcloth or buckskin leggings, certainly a breastplate of bone or a jacket with delicate beadwork, moccasins (again adorned in delicate bead or quill work), and carrying a sacred pipe, tomahawk, bow and arrows, or spear, parfleche, or other conventional regalia. Just to make sure that the Indians he photographed would fit the Noble Savage image, photographer Edward Curtis sometimes carried with him a full set of such standard Plains Indian regalia to dress his subjects of whatever tribe or custom, regardless of what their traditional clothing might have been. The Noble Savage usually looks off toward the heavens, or across a landscape bathed in sunset; he is a departing visionary, a wise and retiring nobleman of the plains or forest, "disembodied through the very glamour of images."[10]

Exoticism, as it is infused into the image of the Noble Savage, tends to mythologize the topical, to essentialize diversity, and to hold its images outside of history as icons of an essential romantic type. In portraying Indians thusly, exoticism transforms them into a moment of nostalgia always receding into the past, which seems, in fact, the basis for most primitivism and millenarianism, whose impossible fantasies lie either in an idealized past or a paradisical future. *Utopia*, it should be remembered, is Latin for "nowhere." As Barthes has further queried, "How does one assimilate the Negro, the Russian? There is here a figure for emergencies: exoticism. The Other becomes a pure object, a spectacle, a clown."[11] The wide commercial use of the Koshare, or clown kachina, one of many available Puebloan Indian images, in art produced by the Taos Society artists and others from the 1920s to the present, perhaps attests to this tendency.

The Noble Savage type lends itself to other appropriations and inflections as well. Its embodiment as an eternal type, for instance, reinforces the notion that the Indian is a relic of the past. This provides further insinuations that Indians exist(ed) only in the past, as a vanishing or vanished race, or that their collective imago, as fixed in the public imagination, should exist only in the nostalgic past, frozen forever in what Berkhofer refers to as the "ethnological present," or in the words of Baudrillard, "frozen, cryogenized, sterilized, protected to death, they have become referential simulacra."[12] "The media," says Stephen Trimble, "continues to do its best to make all Indians the same and then to freeze them in the 'traditional times' of 1880."[13] The Noble Savage as a nostalgic ideal serves only to facilitate such regressive attitudes toward Indians.

In addition, the "mystic warrior" and other subtypes of the Noble Savage make the appropriation of Indianness easier for those who wish to capitalize on this conception. New Age culture in particular has occasioned a resurgence of "plastic medicine men" who reinforce the mystic warrior image for their own capitalistic use, selling Indian religious experiences (such as "vision quest" and "sweat lodge" ceremonies) on the open, often New Age, market, mostly to whites, with little regard for either the sanctity of traditional shamanism or its ceremonial purposes. The American Indian Movement (AIM) has issued a powerful warning against such impostors, whose appropriation of Indian spirituality relies heavily on the public conception of the Noble Savage. One example of how fatuous a reading New Agers can give to traditional Indian spirituality is a spate of recent occurrences at Chaco Canyon, New Mexico, and Mesa Verde National Park, Colorado, both ancestral homes of the Anasazi, progenitors of the southwestern Puebloan tribes. On one occasion, a New Age group filled a kiva at Mesa Verde and barred other visitors from the area while they performed chanting and drumming ceremonies. On others, at Chaco, similar groups have defaced ancient petroglyphs with their own "magic" scrawlings: "They take things, move things, and leave crystals, feathers, and cremated human remains," testified a park superintendent. "At worst, these ceremonies desecrate the places," said Alan Downer, historic preservation director for the Navajo Nation. "At the least, they belittle Native tradition."[14]

The recurrent iconography of both non-Indian and Indian pictorial artists also draws substantially from this stereotype, as ubiquitous today as it was in the 1930s. One need only attend such events as the Denver Indian Market to witness the proliferation of Noble Savage and mystic warrior images for sale. "I shall flee the next Indian art show where the grand prize goes to an Indian painter whose only idea of Indian art is a picture of someone transformed into an eagle," protests an imaginary participant in Rennard Strickland's essay "Tall Visitor at the Indian Gallery." "To whites, that is Indian art!"[15] Crow-Blackfeet artist Susan Steward agrees, saying, "We are often thought of as not contributing much to the mainstream [of art], and the few contributions that are recognized are thought of as quaint or [as supporting] the 'mystic warrior syndrome.'"[16]

Whether clothed (or unclothed) in the ignoble rags of depravity and stupidity or the grand costumes of sanguine nobility, Indians as they have existed in both the fictive and official imagination of the United States have been prisoners of linguistic and psychological projection, just as they have been literal prisoners of the dominant culture. As a result, the identity of the individual and collective Indian throughout postcontact history has been largely one of manipulation and schematic Other destruction. That the design of the white hegemony against Indians has had at its heart the ultimate intention of either cultural or physical genocide can hardly be denied. That the Indian has bitterly resisted such intentions, through the various strategies of warfare, the signing of (now broken) treaties, resigned relocation to reservations, religious conversion, legal recourse, economic savvy, retribalization, political activism, and demythologization, is nothing short of heroic. Central to their fight for cultural autonomy is the realization that Indian stereotypes, whether noble or ignoble, must be defused, both internally within Indian communities and individual psyches, and externally through critical theory, vigilant demythologization, and a resurgence of Indian "autohistories" and individuated Indian voices in the arts and literature, as well as in politics. As we have seen, both literature and art have surreptitiously abetted the saga of colonialism by the perpetuation of stereotypes. Beginning in the 1880s, some literature and art became part of the revolution/revulsion against stereotypes, a reversal whose practitioners are the subjects of the following chapters.

portraits of dishonor

4

Look upon your hands! They are stained by the blood of your relations.
Helen Hunt Jackson's inscription, borrowed from Benjamin Franklin,
in copies of her book A Century of Dishonor, *delivered by her to*
U.S. congressmen in 1880

While the identity of the American Indian was being shaped and constructed by forces emanating from the American government in Washington and its religious allies, the literary world responded with a somewhat more sympathetic voice that reinforced the ideas of paternalism and Christian missionary morality, however self-serving. Euramerican writers not exalting the expansionist view of Manifest Destiny were few among journalists, illustrators, and fiction writers. Longfellow's *Song of Hiawatha* (1855) and James Fenimore Cooper's *Last of the Mohicans* and *The Leatherstocking Tales* (1826–41) remain notable exceptions that tried to assume an empathy with Indian subjects facing the encroachment of the white man. The publication of Helen Hunt Jackson's *A Century of Dishonor* in 1880 and *Ramona* in 1884 also marked a daring departure from the usual depictions of Indians as the accursed Other in American politics and fiction. These works, however, promoted other stereotypes that, while certainly painting Indians in a more compassionate light, still tended to deprive them of any realistic cultural autonomy.

Jackson, a lifelong friend and protégé of Emily Dickinson, was born Helen Fiske Hunt in Dickinson's Amherst, Massachusetts, where she and Dickinson were childhood playmates. She left Amherst in 1844 for school elsewhere in Massachusetts and in New York City, marrying U.S. Army Lieutenant Edward Bissell Hunt in 1852. After the tragic deaths of her husband and her only son, Jackson ventured west for health reasons, marrying William S. Jackson, a founder and leading member of Colorado College in Colorado Springs, in 1875. Jackson and Dickinson maintained their relationship over the years, both by mail and through the mediation of mutual friends, and Jackson was possibly the only person who ever told Dickinson that she was a "a great poet," while Dickinson "read Jackson's work with a reverence she reserved for Shakespeare."[1] It seems evident in *Ramona* that the two women shared a common sensitivity toward their fellow human beings, though it must be said that Jackson's sentimentality in religious matters was not shared by Dickinson, while both exhibited a buffering of sentimentality in their perceptions of social injustice.

Jackson's interest in Indian affairs was sparked by a lecture delivered by Standing Bear, chief of the disenfranchised Ponca tribe, before the Boston Indian Citizenship Committee in 1879. The Ponca were "removed" from their Nebraska ancestral homeland to Indian Territory (now Oklahoma). Standing Bear was imprisoned in 1879 as he and sixty-five members of his tribe attempted to return to Nebraska to bury Standing Bear's son, who died on the long march to Oklahoma. In an illustrious trial, Standing Bear and the Poncas were granted legal status as "human beings" by Federal District Judge Elmer S. Dundy, and public sympathy for them resulted in their restoration to their reservation on the Niobrara River. Inspired by the success of public outcry on the Poncas' behalf, Jackson undertook a year's study of Indian affairs in the archives of the Astor Library in New York City, the culmination of which was *A Century of Dishonor*. The book chronicles the histories of contact of various tribes with white settlers and their treatment up to the time of its writing. Much of the material was gleaned from documents generated by the War Department and the Department of the Interior themselves, and carries a veritable embarrassment of political intrigue and outright fraud. Jackson's arguments for Indian sovereignty and "right of occupancy" of their land, however, fell largely on deaf ears in Washington, though she bound the first volumes "in blood-red cloth" and delivered them at her own expense to all members of Congress.[2]

Jackson continued to work on behalf of Indian rights up until her death in 1885, and considered that work the avocation of her life. "When she died, she said, the word 'Indians' would be found engraved on her brain."[3] After an eighteen-month tour of the Mission Indian villages of California, Jackson wrote her most famous work, *Ramona*.

FATHER SALVIERDERRA'S DREAM

Ramona is in many ways a morality tale that can be favorably compared to Harriet Beecher Stowe's *Uncle Tom's Cabin* (1852) both in intent and effect. While Stowe was responding to the imprecation made to her by her sister-in-law, Mrs. Edward Beecher, that "if I could use a pen as you can, I would write something that would make this whole nation feel what an accursed thing slavery is," Jackson was acting in the same spirit concerning the fate of the Mission Indians of southern California.[4] The historical facts behind Jackson's canonization of the Spanish missionaries' treatment of the California Indians, however, leave Jackson's sentimental portrayal of these Indians in the realm of romantic fantasy, however much her sentiments do humanize her Indian characters and her observations of their mistreatment resound as viable social commentary.

The Spanish Mission period in California is treated nostalgically by Jackson as an era in which Indians were mercifully converted to Christianity and given happy and meaningful work on mission properties, rather like a pre-abolitionist Southern plantation is romanticized in Stowe's work. Jackson evokes a scenario in which "thousands and thousands of Indians [were] all working so happy and peaceful at the Mission" in an aura of idealized paternalism.[5] I will not go further into the similarities between these two works, except to say that they both project upon their respective nonwhite subjects an inflexion of martyrdom largely derived from their Christian perspectives on the ostensible moral "value" of suffering at the hands of the dominant whites.

The historical background of the Mission Indians of California begins with the founding of San Diego in 1769 by Gaspar de Portola and the Franciscan Father Junipero Serra. As Carl Waldman notes in his *Encyclopedia of Native American Tribes*, "A military man and a priest often traveled together so that both state and church were represented," and such was the case throughout the Spanish conquest of the American Southwest (by Coronado) as well as of the Southeast (by Ponce de León), Mexico (by Cortés), and of Central and South America.

> Junipero Serra stayed on in California and founded many more missions along with other Franciscans—21 in the coastal region

between San Diego and San Francisco. The Indians they mission-
ized had been peaceful hunter-gatherers, living in tune with their
plentiful environment. But soldiers at the missions' neighboring
presidios (forts) rounded them up and forced them to live at the
missions. The friars taught them to speak Spanish and to practice
the Catholic religion. They also taught them to tend fields, vine-
yards, and livestock, as well as how to make adobe and soap. Then
they were forced to work—to build churches and to produce food.
If the Indians refused or ran away and were caught, they received
whippings as punishment. . . . Before long, the Indians had lost
their own language and religion as well as their tribal identity.[6]

In contrast, Jackson characterizes Fr. Serra as a heroic man destined "to
reclaim the wilderness and its people to his country and church."[7] Following
the closure of the missions in 1834 by the Mexican government came the
Mexican Cession of 1848 and the California Gold Rush of the next year, all
of which further disempowered and dislocated Indians and brought on a
tidal wave of white settlers and gold seekers, who eventually got title to
much of what was traditionally Indian land. One of these tribes, now only
named by what the Spanish called them, because their Native name has
been forever forgotten, were the Luiseño, who are the Indian subjects of
Jackson's novel.

    As we have already noticed, negative and positive stereotypes often con-
front and play off each other in the portrayal of the Indian, and such is the
case in *Ramona* as well. The story centers on a faltering Mexican *ranchería,*
whose misguided matron, the Señora Moreno, has taken in her older sister's
adopted child, a "half-breed" named Ramona Ortegna. Ramona is not privy
to her mixed heritage, though Sra. Moreno and others of the older guard are,
so she lives the first part of her life in naive bliss as a señorita of the
household. Jackson uses Ramona's ignorance of her Indian nature to show
how racial prejudices and ideologies involve the still prevalent, pseudoscien-
tific notions of genetic inferiority based on bloodlines, which in turn produced a racial ideology that tyrannized all peoples who did not have the
"pure" bloodlines of the dominant race. This social Darwinism eventually
led to the concept of eugenics and promoted the concept that racial purity
was the sine qua non of social evolution, and that a mixing of the bloodlines
would result in devolution and the appearance of the atavistic, if not bestial,

characteristics commonly attributed to, in this instance, Indians. If one does not know one's bloodline is "tainted," however, as is the case with Ramona, then racism cannot exist. That most "Mexicans" such as Sra. Moreno were historically of mixed race, part Spanish and part Indian (mestizos), is not alluded to here but suggests one of the great ironies of racism.

Like the "mulatto" of African-American literature, the half-breed Ramona serves to signify a true Other who is neither white like her father, a Scot, nor Indian like her mother. She is thus a true vessel, or alembic, in and through whom Jackson can demonstrate her own liberal feelings about the "blood" or authentic substance of Indianness versus that of whiteness. In so doing, she illuminates both the stereotype of the romanticized Indian princess (the result of her sympathy with her characters) and that of the brute Indian (the result of her observations concerning prevailing social views). The central tension of the work is between Ramona's Indianness and her whiteness, a battle for identity fought thematically between the Sra. Moreno, for the latter, and the full-blooded Indian Alessandro Assis, for the former; but the battle is ultimately fought within the heart of Ramona herself.

The romanticized nature of Ramona is evident from the beginning of the novel. She seems indeed the epitome of *la belle sauvage*. When she meets the old Franciscan monk who knew her in her childhood, the monk's impression of this now adolescent Ramona is tellingly sublime and reverential: "She had looked to the devout old monk, as she sprang through the cloud of golden flowers, the sun falling on her bared head, her cheeks flushed, her eyes shining, more like an apparition of an angel or saint, than like the flesh and blood maiden he had carried in his arms when she was a babe." The heavily romanticized illustration accompanying the 1884 text, by N. C. Wyeth, promotes the ambiance of blithe spirituality and sensuality. Father Salvierderra further notes the exotic beauty of her mixed racial heritage, thinking to himself that "she had just enough of olive tint in her complexion to underlie and enrich her skin without making it swarthy," in which characterization one senses a subtle paean to the prospect of appropriating from Indians just enough of their identity so as to enliven and enrich the paternal race aesthetically, as some Romantic French painters often did on canvas (for example Delacroix, Ingres, and the British painter Benjamin West).[8]

Such depictions of the ethereal Indian princess hark back to the eighteenth century, as does this one by explorer William Bird in *Histories of the Dividing Line* (1728): "Her complexion was a deep Copper so that her fine Shape & regular Features made her appear like a statue in Bronze done by a masterly Hand."[9] They also carry over into the 1900s, as in Carl Sandburg's poem "Cool Tombs" (1918), wherein we find "Pocahontas' body, lovely as a poplar, Sweet as a red/haw in November, or a paw paw in May."[10] Pocahontas-like figures also waltzed across the American stage in several incarnations, from J. N. Barker's lavishly romanticized *The Indian Princess; or La Belle Sauvage* in 1808 to John Brougham's "popular burlesque" *Po-Ca-Han-Tas* in 1918. Jackson, of course, takes her stereotype seriously as a martyr to the Indian cause.

While Jackson idealizes her Ramona, she also reveals the meanness and hypocrisy of the paternalistic attitude that pervaded the mission paradigm. When the charismatic Alessandro, a full-blooded Luiseño sheepshearer, appears on the ranchería, the Sra. Moreno, thinking to hire him full-time, refuses to consider "the possibility of an Indian's being so born and placed that he would hesitate about becoming permanently a servant."[11] Sra. Moreno, casting herself as a representative of the cult of Mary, the Franciscan clergy, and the Mexican aristocracy, embodies the several views of the Indian that facilitated and justified their "destiny" as a slavish and inferior race. "Naked savages they themselves too, to-day [*sic*], if we had not come here to teach and civilize them," she snorts. "The race was never meant for anything but servants."[12] Perhaps most telling in this respect is the following passage:

> "[Ramona] may be ill; but people do not die of love like hers for Alessandro."
>
> "Of what kind do they die, mother?" asked Felipe, impatiently.
>
> The Señora looked reproachfully at him. "Not often of any," she said; "but certainly not of a sudden passion for a person in every way beneath them, in position, in education, in all points which are essential to *congeniality* of tastes or association of life."
>
> The Señora spoke calmly, with no excitement, *as if she were discussing an abstract case.*[13]

The Señora's evocation of a "congeniality of tastes" brings to mind the drive for homogeneity from which stereotypes are made, and the narrator's feeling that she is "discussing an abstract case" emphasizes the distance between Alessandro as he might actually be and the presumptuous "simulation" that she has made of him.

Jackson as narrator tries to be more magnanimous, but we can still hear, couched in her more "liberal" authorial voice, a condescension that bespeaks the times. "But he was not a civilized man," she writes of Alessandro; "he had to bring to bear on his present situation only simple, primitive, uneducated instincts and impulses."[14] These are traits that Jackson admires, nonetheless, though her admiration hardly softens the sting of Christian prejudice. The notion that all Indians were heathen ripe for conversion to a more civil and proper Christian life carries within it the darker impulses to enslave and subsume an alien culture. No matter how well-meaning the Spanish and Anglo missionaries and *patrones* might have been, and that is certainly open to argument, the Christianizing mechanisms for conversion still required that the alien race or culture be dehumanized. Another of the señora's ranch hands, Juan Canito, speaks of "those beasts of Indians"; "it is a good thing for those poor Indian devils to get a bit of religion now and then," he says on another occasion.[15]

As the story unfolds, Ramona falls in love with Alessandro, a situation that the embittered señora cannot abide. She tells her son, Felipe, who has grown to love Ramona both as an adopted sister and as a potential wife, "If you had a sister, you would rather see her dead than married to any one of these Indians," and torments him with the probability that should Ramona go against her and marry Alessandro, they would both be driven from the ranch. Indeed they do marry and in their exile become akin to Christian martyrs in the romanticization of their plight.

Since Ramona is forced to choose for her identity "an alien's position," as the señora puts it, she must now live the marginalized life of the Other, ostracized against all reason, beyond the help of the paternal church or the maternal ranch. She is now fully an Indian, and as such both she and Alessandro are hunted for horse stealing; Alessandro's village is forfeit to forged Anglo land claims; their child dies, ostensibly because Ramona "had offended the Virgin and . . . in one short hour the Virgin had punished her"; and, after further travail, Alessandro is gunned down in front of his own house.[16] Jackson parlays the tragedy into an epiphany of Christian morality, for as Alessandro is dying,

> Ramona rose, went into the house, brought out the white altar-cloth, and laid it over the mutilated face. As she did this, she recalled words she had heard Father Salvierderra quote as having been said by Father Junipero, when one of the Franciscan Fathers

had been massacred by the Indians, at San Diego. "Thank God!" he said, "the ground is now watered by the blood of a martyr!"[17]

The local sheriff would do nothing, for "to betray sympathy for Indians was more than any man's political head was worth."[18] In previous passages, as well, the spiritual superiority of Alessandro is alluded to by Jackson, wherein he becomes aligned with the mystic warrior stereotype. Early on, he magically cures Felipe of a long illness by building him a special bed and playing the violin for him. Juan Canito notes his "native amiability and sweetness," and the narrator concludes that "when it came to the things of the soul, and of honor, Alessandro's plane was the higher."[19]

Indeed, both Alessandro and Ramona are well thought of by the narrator, the priests, and most other parties in the novel. Jackson humanizes both of them through the manipulation of her stereotypes to serve the cause of the Indian, but principally that of the converted Indian. Significantly, the only mention of drunkenness occurs among white traders, never in regard to the Indian characters. Jackson also offers several lucid instances that portray the real plight of Indians. As Alessandro complains to the good father, "They say the Americans, when they buy the Mexicans' lands, drive the Indians away as if they were dogs; they say we have no right to our lands."[20] The historical issue of the theft of Indian land resounds throughout the book, as do those of the mistreatment and murder of Indian peasants and the issue of assimilation. At one point, Ramona suggests to Alessandro that they go to Los Angeles and live in the white culture—"What does Majella [Alessandro's pet name for her] think would become of one Indian, or two, alone among the whites? If they will come to our villages and drive us out a hundred at a time, what would they do to one man alone?"

> No man will pay an Indian but half wages. . . . And now they pay the Indians in money sometimes, half wages; sometimes in bad flour, or things he does not want; sometimes in whiskey. . . . One man in San Bernardino last year, when an Indian would not take a bottle of sour wine for pay for a day's work, shot him in the cheek with his pistol, and told him to mind how he was insolent any more.[21]

Ramona remains, despite its effulgent romanticism, nostalgia, and paucity of social realism, the first fictive account by a white author to take the

Indian side of the American colonial racial question. By constructing stereo-types on both sides, Jackson provides us with a morality play that both patronizes and honors Indian characters. Her awareness of the social and economic plight of Indians—as exemplified by her attentiveness to the prob-lems of assimilation, land grabbing, miscegenation, mixed-bloods, reserva-tion politics, and racial prejudice—make her work exceptional for its time. Jackson also emphasizes the growing confusion about "authentic" Indian identities, and authenticity based on racial blood-typing is dealt with in a serious way. The book's greatest failing is that it does little to help us under-stand Indians as they lived within their own culture, and even less to accen-tuate the historical tragedy that lay, in the missions, at the feet of Christian capitalism and expansionism. The converted Indian, such as those envi-sioned by Father Salvierderra, is the nostalgic icon, and *Ramona* finally holds out hope only for a "new dispensation, in which the Mission establishments should be reinstated in all their old splendor and prosperity, and their Indian converts again numbered by tens of thousands."[22] Such a future is probably not the utopian dream of most Indians living today.

a recapitulation of indianness   5

I forgot the gods then. I followed the Jesus trail.
  "Came With War"

If Christian sentimentality formulated the stereotyped Indians in *Ramona* and made them martyrs in a more or less Christian allegory about prejudice and racial purity, we find quite the opposite in *Laughing Boy* (1929), a romantic portrayal of Indian culture and religion that pits itself against Christian influences. Oliver La Farge, like other great dramatists, saw the literary and political value of posing a countermyth against the master myth of the ruling culture. By personifying his Indian Others and grounding them in a meaningful cosmology separate from that of Christian culture, La Farge creates a powerful antidote to the "alien" nature of the Other—he makes his a deeply human hero, adored by gods and humans alike. If Christianity has generally viewed Indians principally as heathens, besotted by false gods and primitive notions, and has thus sought to void them of their Indianness on these grounds, through conversion or extirpation, then what better means to combat that process than by filling Indianness with its own substantial mythos, enforced by "real," active gods who, in this novel, have the ostensible power of the "Slayer of Enemy Gods"? With a charismatic Indian protagonist, Laughing Boy, and his Christian-tainted wife, Slim Girl, caught up in a Pulitzer Prize–winning tale of cultural warfare, La Farge has written a landmark work that ennobles and humanizes Indians and begins the literary turn from stereotypical to archetypal characterization.

However, as Win Blevins has noted, "In *Laughing Boy* . . . Navajo life still seems a kind of pastoral idyll, a Rousseauian tribute to a natural life that must be viewed nostalgically."[1] This criticism is underscored by La Farge's own hand. He writes in his foreword, for instance, that "this book was written about a people who have now vanished" by a writer (whom La Farge purports to have known) who was "ferocious [and] romantic at the same time."[2] Such a statement, which sounds ingenuous and contrived today, still enunciates the lingering stereotype of the Noble Savage that plays out in the text: ferocious and romantic. The notion of a "vanishing breed" is one of the standard criteria for deciding whether a fictive work relies on Indian stereotypes; by portraying Indians as an "extinct species," an author reinforces the nonexistence of Indian culture as a present and therefore tangible reality. While such a posture is more onerous today, it was somewhat less so at the time La Farge was living among and writing about the Navajo. As D'Arcy McNickle points out, "[La Farge's] first association with Indians in the United States occurred in a period when cultural and biological extinction seemed imminent and inevitable," largely due to the real precariousness of their situation and a general apathy on the part of the American government.[3] Certainly La Farge's forty-year dedication to the welfare and continued existence of American Indians precludes any conscious attempt on his part to undermine their cultural and political reality.

La Farge also dissembles that "this story is meant neither to instruct nor to prove a point, but to amuse," a claim that belies the effect of the work, which is highly polemical and acutely antiwhite.[4] Such affectation, of course, eases white readers into the problems confronted in the story by making them think they are to be amused, rather charmed, by what one unnamed *Saturday Review* critic called a "long story of primitive love in which the story complex is so completely kept within its native color and tone," which is to say: it is an Indian curiosity not to be taken as important literature.[5] From La Farge's, and McNickles's, point of view, "The problem was, somehow, to bring all that he knew about the Navajo people into a rational universe, to project them in their proper human form unencumbered by their habits of behavior and custom which made them picturesque but savage in the eyes of outsiders."[6] Despite the fact that La Farge himself later regretted the youthful and somewhat naive romanticism that pervades the novel, *Laughing Boy* still serves as a landmark novel of Indian characterization.

The time of the novel ("romanticism made him [the fictitious author] feel that he should cast back in time to a less corrupted, purer era, so he chose 1915 as the date of his story") lends itself to some historical scrutiny.[7] It was a time when the American Southwest was becoming that most idealized locale, "the Land of Enchantment," and images of the Indian were appearing everywhere to market it as such for the burgeoning tourist trade. Perhaps foremost among its advertisers was the Santa Fe branch of the Atchison, Topeka and Santa Fe Railway (AT&SF). The great westering spirit of American entrepreneurship was abetted by a national longing for the grandeur of the West as inspired by painters such as Alfred Bierstadt and Thomas Moran, and by poets such as Whitman, who wrote prophetically in 1871 about his own westering spirit: "I see over my own continent the Pacific railroad surmounting every barrier / . . . / I hear the locomotives rushing and roaring, and the shrill steam-whistle / I hear the echoes reverberate through the grandest scenery in the world."[8] And the AT&SF obliged, completing its penetration of New Mexico in 1878 by laying rail over Raton Pass.

What followed was a major promotional campaign for tourist traffic into the new territory, called "Indian Detours," which relied heavily on the allure of Native cultures and romantic portrayals of the Indian, reproduced nationwide on calendars and in Santa Fe brochures. The line into New Mexico was named The Chief, and its logo carried a stylized Indian. As T. C. McLuhan observes in her excellent study, *Dream Tracks,* "The Indian became a popular theme in the paintings of these [regional and corporate] artists, even though they knew little about the culture they were 'capturing.' "[9] Significantly, Laughing Boy and Slim Girl set up their household along these very same "dream tracks" in the fictional town of Los Palos, and make their living by crafting traditional Indian jewelry and weaving for the tourist trade. This incursion of the white tourist/settler-colonist into the ostensible sanctity of Indian culture is the catalyst of the novel's tragedy.

"The attraction [to artists] was twofold," continues McLuhan:

> The Indians' unity with their natural environment as expressed through their religious ceremonials and daily life stirred the spirit and aroused the curiosity of the artist. In addition, their colorful

and picturesque appearance and strange and exotic customs provided a strong visual stimulus.[10]

The works produced during this heyday, mostly by transplanted European
and East Coast illustrators, painters, and printmakers, are some of the most
elegant and colorful of any American art. The famous "New Mexico light"
and the uniqueness of the desert landscape, coupled with the exoticism of
Indian subjects, made for very romantic and dramatic compositions, whose
use of the Indian as subject is discussed more extensively in chapter 6. Most of
these painters aspired to a painterly ethereality like that of the great French
and German romantic painters of the previous century: Ingres, Delacroix,
and Friedrich. They could easily have been illustrators for La Farge's novel,
whose language verges on the poetic and the mystical, as does his theme.

Laughing Boy (whose Indian name is "Sings Before Spears") and Slim
Girl ("Came With War") live steeped in the mysticism and ceremonial
religion of traditional Navajo life as observed directly by La Farge, an eastern
intellectual who nonetheless lived in and studied the culture extensively. His
perceptions of its predicament reveal him to be an informed and deeply

conscious observer, and carry weight unto the present day. "Most Indians, I believe, want to retain their identity," La Farge wrote in the Methodist magazine, *Together*, in 1958.

> They do not want to be assimilated or to have their tribes and rights as Indians terminated. This desire to continue as Indians does not mean wanting to stay primitive, wear feathers, or live in tents. It is based on the idea that men can be different yet progress equally.

Though this attitude is perhaps more mature than the one he held during the writing of *Laughing Boy*, it is nonetheless one that announces the ambivalence of Laughing Boy the character. From 1926 to 1929, during which time he wrote the novel, La Farge's impetus was more romantic and less concerned with the political survival of the Navajo, whom he viewed at the time in terms similar to those of poet Gary Snyder in 1969: "up to your hips in Gods / your head all turned to eagle-down / & lightning for knees and elbows / your eyes full of pollen."[11] They also inhabit a landscape of sublime, painterly beauty:

> Right before their horses' feet the cliff fell away, some fourteen hundred feet, and there, under their hands, lay all the North Country. It was red in the late sunlight, fierce, narrow cañons with ribbons of shadow, broad valleys and lesser hills streaked with purple opaque shadows like deep holes in the world, cast by the upthrust mesas. The great, black volcanic core of Agathla was a somber monstrosity in the midst of colour. Away and away it stretched, jumbled, vast, the crazy shapes of the Monuments, the clay hills of Utah, and far beyond everything, floating blue mountain shapes softer than the skies.[12]

While such description certainly has a ring of authenticity to it, it also partakes of the romantic grandeur of the "land of enchantment," a term used in the novel itself, meant to reinforce the surreal nature of the Indian characters and their culture.

Reflecting somewhat the sentimentality of Jackson, La Farge attempts to create Indian characters who embody the pastoral and idyllic simplicity of the Noble Savage. "It is the essence of pastoral life," exudes the narrator. "Cigarette smoke rises lazily in the hot air, the sun is comfortable upon one's bones, the gently moving animals make peace."[13] Laughing Boy and Slim Girl imagine and act out an elegantly simple life together—he a silversmith, she a weaver—"to complete her idyll, she wanted to weave."[14] She sees in Laughing Boy the mystic warrior stereotype that La Farge makes of him in part, a character who, like Alessandro in *Ramona,* has the innate charm and power of the supernatural. It is Laughing Boy who embodies the untainted purity of the ancient ways, who maintains the mythic force of the Navajo "path of beauty" and walks with the gods. He is "that imperious warrior who gave her [Slim Girl] orders. . . . a religious man, schooled to obedience of absolute conventions."[15] La Farge has partly fashioned Laughing Boy from one of the sacred twins of Navajo legend, Nayenezgani, "whose name signifies Slayer of the Alien Gods," an important and powerful personage in the origin legend (Diné bahana) of the Navajos as recounted by Washington Matthews in 1897.[16] He is also one of the "copper gods" (as Ramona was), replete with the physique that La Farge idealizes in his Indian boys, with "slender, golden-brown bodies, the bodies of perfect boys."[17] He is an exemplar of The People, or Diné, as the Navajo call themselves. What La Farge hopes to do here, however romanticized, is to portray a culture that has an autonomous religious history and identity that is not in need of conversion. In addition, as I will discuss later, Laughing Boy and Slim Girl are also three-dimensional, humanized Indians who go about the everyday business of living in a very casual and believable way; they are portrayed as ambiguous and complex human beings.

The story of Laughing Boy and Slim Girl is, again, the story of two cultures locked in the battle of racial ideologies. While Laughing Boy and traditional Navajo culture assume a central power here, Slim Girl, on the other hand, is cursed by her affiliation with white American culture, try as she might to escape its corrupting influence and go "back to the blanket" via her love for Laughing Boy. Several historical resonances appear in the story that highlight the tragic Indian policies of the government in "Washing-don," as it is referred to by Slim Girl. She is one of the thousands of Indians who were taken from their homes and heritages, often by force, and sent to "away schools" run by the white government under the auspices of the BIA. "By 1913," writes Trimble, "the eight BIA boarding schools on the [Navajo] reservation—in addition to more distant off-reservation schools and several mission schools—began educating hundreds of Navajos in Anglo ways."[18] The idea that Indians must become assimilated into Euramerican culture rather than practice their own traditional lifeways was, like conversion, based on the assumption that Indians as Indians were undesirable to the Christian hegemony, and the schools sought to void their students of Indianness. Underhill bemoans the effects of away schools on Indian boys who, denied their traditional vision quests, "were made to feel inadequate in their new tasks, their energy and ambition went down to zero and generations have been needed to bring it up."[19]

As Slim Girl recalls, " 'They did not want us to be Indians. . . . They wanted us to be ashamed of being Indians. They wanted us to forget our mothers and fathers.' "[20] Trying to be an "American," Slim Girl "forgot the gods then, [and] followed the Jesus trail."[21] She then got pregnant by a white man who refused to marry her, leading her to become abandoned by the priest who converted her. Slim Girl found herself in the company of whores, who took her in and cared for her; she became a whore, hoping someday to avenge herself on the white ways that corrupted her: "I made up my mind that an American should pay for what an American had done."[22] Her love for Laughing Boy is her only hope for restoring herself to the People, but, in her quest for material security and revenge, she continues to service sexually another white rancher while she is married to Laughing Boy, and is discovered. Although Laughing Boy forgives her, and they begin their journey away from the "dream tracks" back into their own culture, she is murdered on the way, becoming a somewhat stereotypical victim of American corruption. Like another character, Yellow Singer, who becomes an alcoholic thanks to American whiskey, Slim Girl is the epitome of the corrupted Indian who has wandered from the traditional "path of beauty" and dies from the machinations of the alien mythos of white Christendom, which now pervades the otherwise "pure" mythos of Indianness like "something in the air, something that perverted the world."[23] White Americans are known to the Indians appropriately as "The Hunger People."

Through the figure of Laughing Boy, the Navajo "way" emerges as a magical realm in which nature and the supernatural are conjoined and indistinguishable. La Farge's hozoji, more correctly *hózhǫ́*, is and was at the center of Navajo mythology, as witnessed by Washington Matthews in 1897 and before. Matthews translated *hozó* to mean "terrestrial beauty," and its derivative *hozógo* to mean "in a beautiful earthly manner."[24] It is currently thought to "embrace wholeness, life force, rootedness in the Earth, completeness, and 'continuous generational animation.' "[25] Thus Laughing Boy is portrayed as constantly praying in the spirit of hozoji (*hózhǫ́ǫ́jí*), the Blessingway ceremony: "'Now with a god I walk, / Striding across the foothills. / Now on the old age trail, now on the path of beauty wandering. / In beauty—Hozoji, hozoji, hozoji, hozoji-i, hozoji," echoing the ages old "Prayer of Beauty" from the Navajo Night Chant.[26] But there is also a constant questioning as to the power of hozoji to oppose the white man's "magic": "He walked to and fro. My mind is made up, I shall make things as they should be. Now with a god I walk—or is it a game, looseness?"[27] In the context of this novel, the identity of the Indian protagonist is not to be consigned wholly to either racial or religious stereotypes, nor is his fate linked to any determinant religious program, even that of his own tribe.

Details of Laughing Boy's day-to-day existence and his personality also defy the stereotypical mystic warrior image we and Slim Girl might have of him. He is, in many ways, just an Indian boy doing Indian things that have less to do with a grand mythos than with the mundane business of life: he herds and cares for his horses, drinks coffee with too much sugar, smokes the traditional cigarette, gets drunk enough times to teach himself not to, gambles and races horses ("an acknowledged Indian road to success"[28]), enjoys attacking and even killing "Pah-Utes" (Paiutes) and is not above intertribal rivalries, plays sly tricks on American tourists and traders, and in general is far from being an idealized, omnipotent character capable of slaying the "enemy gods." In the end, he cannot even save Slim Girl, who had hoped to "make a god of him" as part of her revenge against white culture.[29]

There is an ambivalence about Laughing Boy's character, and about hozoji itself, wherein we discover the more archetypal Indian individual who, like the kachina dancers who impersonate the gods during ceremonial dances, are "just Indians . . . dressed up in a rather silly way," as Slim Girl puts it; "all of them knew that the gods were no more than men in masks."[30] Although Laughing Boy "loved the gatherings of people, the huge fires, the holy things," he also believed that "what he had was so vastly superior to anything in their philosophy."[31] This ambivalence regarding the traditional myths and ceremonies suggests that within both of these characters more archetypal, self-defining forces are at play, forces that emerge from "inside" their personas as intentional attempts at personal authenticity. La Farge has evoked a largely accurate and powerful Indian mythos only to engage us in a personification of believable Indian characters. This strategy, rather than the Olympian intervention of a supernatural masked god, is what dismantles white racial ideology so convincingly in *Laughing Boy*. We realize that the Indian Laughing Boy, like us, is just an all-too-human actor in the strange pageant of life, a more psychologically accurate expression of the human dilemma of identity. Upon the death of Slim Girl, Laughing Boy discovers in himself that "now he was not a Navajo terrified of the dead, not an Indian, not an individual of any race, but a man who had buried his own heart."[32] His presumed identity is thus shaken by an "archetype of meaning" (death) that Jung suggests surfaces when

> we are caught and entangled in aimless experience, and the judging intellect with all its categories proves itself powerless. Human interpretation fails, for a turbulent life-situation has arisen that refuses to fit any of the traditional meanings assigned to it. It is a moment of collapse.[33]

Such collapse, in Jungian theory, signifies the beginnings of individuation; in literature, it signifies an attempt to humanize and elevate Indian characters through the dramatic process of tragedy. Laughing Boy, returning to a ceremonial after five days of fasting and prayer at the grave of Slim Girl, finds at last that "the past and present came together, he was one with himself. The good and true things he had thought entered into his being and were part of the whole continuity of his life."[34] Clearly he is a fully articulated fictional Indian, who surpasses any previous depictions in white-generated American literature.

One stereotype giveaway is the lack of faithful transliteration of Indian dialect and/or the granting to Indian characters a speech that is not merely gibberish or pidgin English. "Do the People speak in 'early jawbreaker' or in the oratorical style of the 'noble savage'?" is one of the criteria of Beverly Slapin and Doris Seale, who edited and published the teachers' guide, *Through Indian Eyes: The Native Experience in Books for Children*, in 1992.[35] Stedman asserts that the Navajos' speech in La Farge's novel is "almost exclusively . . . not of the English pattern," and criticizes La Farge's Slim Girl for speaking with "disses" and "dats" to the white rancher she services.[36] Just for the record, Slim Girl and Laughing Boy do speak in this way at times, but only in the presence of whites, and they do so with the conscious intent to conceal their intelligence for their own advantage. All the rest of these characters' language, both verbalized and subvocal, is elegantly simple, poetic, and often full of remarkable insight:

You will see what is left of a man when he leaves our way, when he walks in moccasins on the Americans' road. You have seen other People who live down there. Some of them are rich, but their hearts are empty. You have seen them without happiness or beauty in their hearts, because they have lost the Trail of Beauty. Now they have nothing to put in their hearts except whiskey.[37]

Laughing Boy is emblematic of a more enlightened period in American history, when the ideas of cultural anthropologist Franz Boas were beginning to gain wide acceptance, at least among white intellectuals such as La Farge, who studied anthropology at Harvard and Tulane Universities. Boas stressed "actual history over conjectural history" in his studies of American Indians, believing that Indian cultures ought to be studied as individual paradigms. The terms "cultural relativity" and "pluralism" were initiated by Boas to defuse the notions that white civilization was innately superior to other, "aboriginal" civilizations, and that social evolution, as social Darwinism had earlier insisted, necessarily resulted in a Western social structure. While not as dynamic a shift as it might first appear, Boasian anthropology at least unveiled the heterogeneity among Indian tribes and ascribed to them unique cultural histories, which in some measure led to the dissolution of the stereotypically homogeneous Indian.

This momentum carried into the BIA under the commissionership of John Collier, himself a progressive reformer who fought tirelessly for Native cultural, economic, and political sovereignty during his reign from 1933 to 1945. La Farge, then president of the National Association on Indian Affairs, advised Collier on Navajo, Hopi, and Puebloan aspects of the Indian Reorganization Act of 1934, and shared Collier's desires to institute tribal councils among the tribes of the Southwest. Both were part of the revisioning of the Indian as an autonomous bearer of a valued culture.[38] Certain Navajos were displeased with the accuracy with which La Farge scrutinized and reiterated their cultural ways, a sign that he was of the same mind as Boas regarding explicitly Indian traits and activities. Indeed, in 1930 La Farge was advised by a colleague at the University of Pennsylvania that "Boas recommended you very highly for ethnological research."[39] On the other hand, the publication of *Laughing Boy* catalyzed a new self-interest among Indians who read it and helped inspire a generation of Indian novelists, three of whom—D'Arcy McNickle, John Milton Oskison, and John Joseph Mathews—published major works in the decade following 1929.

the enchantment of the disenfranchised   6

ARTISTIC IMAGES OF THE PUEBLO INDIAN

[T]hey are the possessions of the imaginations of white men, who dress them up for a new game of white and red man, in which the Pueblo Indian, indeed, gets to play the good guy, but only as seen through a pattern of beliefs characteristic of white America.

Julie Schimmel, art professor and author

The "dream tracks" that brought thousands of new whites into the Southwest as tourists also brought a number of artists who, in a close association with the railroad, promoted a thriving art market dealing in images of Indians and their symbolic regalia. Thanks to the clever and aggressive marketing strategies of the Atchison, Topeka & Santa Fe Railroad (AT&SF) and a hotel and restaurant entrepreneur named Fred Harvey, these artists were given a substantial vested interest in portraying Indians as picturesque primitives imbued in a glowing landscape. The romantic elements of exoticism and wilderness locales, the architectural distinctiveness of Puebloan culture, and the cooperation of curious and flattered Indian subjects, not to mention the financial impetus created by tourist trade promoters, all combined to ensure a profusion of pictorial images that both ennobled and exploited Indian cultures.

Because many white Americans living east of the Mississippi had acquired a fearful, tentative impression of the Indian, based on the good Indian/bad Indian literary, political, and pictorial stereotypes prior to the turn of the century, the railroads that ventured toward California in the last decades of the nineteenth century needed a new image to attract customers into Indian Country, which by this time was reservation Indian country, largely confined to the western mountain states. Corporate image makers thus sought to capitalize on the Edenic notions of the Wild West that had also crept into the public imagination via the art of the great landscape painters Bierstadt and Moran, who had already effectively ephemeralized the West, and through the wide exposure "tame" Indians had gotten through such promoters as Buffalo Bill Cody. "It fell on the shoulders of William Haskell Simpson," writes T. C. McLuhan, "Assistant General Passenger Agent for the line and in charge of Santa Fe advertising operations for more than twenty-two years, to lure a nation full of potential customers by instilling an image of 'the people's kind of railroad.'"[1] The Indian was to be made a significant, if unwitting, agent in this seduction.

Simpson was to be a genius in his field. Although it was CEO Edward Ripley who bought and reproduced the first official AT&SF artwork, a scene of the Grand Canyon by Moran, and distributed copies of it widely to advertise the line, Simpson was to become one of corporate America's biggest art patrons. An art lover to begin with, Simpson continued to give free rail travel into the Southwest to any artist who wanted to paint the new territory, a practice that began with Ripley in 1895. While several members of what was to become the Taos Society of Artists (TSA) had already visited New Mexico and were duly impressed with its artistic potential, Simpson was instrumental in luring them to stay in and around Taos and in attracting other neophyte artists into the aura of Indian enchantment. Foremost among these were Ernest L. Blumenschein, Joseph H. Sharp, Eanger Irving Couse, Walter Ufer, Bert Geer Phillips, Oscar Birninghaus, and, although never a TSA member, William R. Leigh. The strange alliance among these artists, Simpson, and Harvey was to produce a major revisioning of the Pueblo Indians, as well as their new denigration into tourist attractions and "collectible" entities.

WILLIAM R. LEIGH

Like La Farge and Frank Waters to follow, William R. Leigh was fascinated enough with Pueblo Indian culture to immerse himself in the day-to-day banalities as well as the ceremonial grandeur of its contemporary reality in the 1920s and 1930s. "In the commonplace scenes of southwestern Indian life Leigh found the content for his finest work," and he found it most especially among the Zuni, Navajo, and Hopi.[2] After his art schooling at the Royal Academy of Fine Arts in Munich, he initially began his career with

portrait painting and illustrating, but did not find immediate success. Wishing to broaden his horizons, and having been impressed by Moran's appeal for "more native art, independent of European fads," Leigh headed out west on one of the Santa Fe Railroad junkets under the auspices of Simpson, who expected a painting of the Grand Canyon out of the deal. "There in New Mexico [at Laguna Pueblo], all the pieces suddenly fell into place."[3] Leigh made some twenty-five trips to the area throughout his productive years. Leigh and Simpson's association was to become typical of that between the railroad and its artists. The railroad bought five of his paintings in 1906, one of which became the cover for the dining-car menu on The Chief line.[4] Though he did not deal exclusively with Simpson after that, Leigh's principal subject matter continued to come from the Southwest.

Leigh was an artist, like Moran, heavily influenced by the French romantic painter Delacroix. A French magazine reviewer noted, six months before Leigh's death, that "in our country he [Leigh] would be compared to Delacroix whose dash and romanticism the American painter often shows."[5]

Navajo Fire Dance (oil, 1943) by William R. Leigh was first sketched in 1939 during a performance of the Navajo Night Chant. (Courtesy of the Woolaroc Museum, Bartlesville, Oklahoma.)

His love for the romantic sublime in nature and his attention to and invocation of atmospherics are also reminiscent of Turner in his later palette-knife paintings. *Rain Clouds, Kayenta, Arizona* (1922), *Sunset* (n.d.), and *Laguna, New Mexico* (n.d.), all sparse landscapes of distant buttes, are nonetheless full of sky, whose air is thick with the electricity of color and motion that recall Turner's *The Battle of Trafalgar*. Despite these romantic leanings, Leigh was able to paint the Indian with much less exoticism than might be expected. Like Taos Society artists Phillips and Ufer, Leigh was genuinely interested in Indian society and managed to expel at least some of his romantic conventions when addressing Indian subjects.

Cummins recounts one instance that characterizes Leigh's obsession with authentic Indian customs. In 1939 he had spent most of nine days and nights with the Navajo during a Night Chant ceremony being held in midwinter under the direst of conditions. As Washington Matthews recalls, these ceremonials, most performed to cure the sick, were "performed only during the coldest part of the year—the months when the snakes are dormant."[6] In the words of Leigh's biographer:

> Long ago he read of the Night Chant [probably in Matthews] and now, late in years, he had risked his health in the dead of winter to be an eye-witness. Freezing on one side, baking on the other [from the roaring fire], with children laughing, shouting, and jumping about, he studied the dance intently. At last, satisfied that all conditions were precise, he took a pencil from his pocket and on the pad in front of him began drawing with loose and heavy strokes.[7]

The result would be the mural-sized *Navajo Fire Dance*, one of his most eloquent works, completed in 1943. The Indian figures, though somewhat angular and assuming some improbable contortions, dance around a large bonfire in stylistic authenticity. The night air is lit with the magic of a full moon half-obscured by a spruce tree and the intensity of the Wright-of-Darby–like fire, epitomizing the sublime fury of nature. In the immediate foreground sit the Navajo attendees, huddled against the cold and the frozen ground. The "serious play" of Navajo ceremonialism intrigues without being overwrought, and the dancing Indians are depicted in the traditional clothing of their own tribe: a red headband/bandanna, midcalf leggings, and breechcloths. That Leigh studied the entire Night Chant, with its 24 episodes and 324 songs, and sat through its entire performance (though only one night of the ceremony is devoted to public dancing), attests to his concern that Indian rituals be portrayed with a Boasian sense of their sacramental importance and not just exploited for their curiosity.

Forcing the viewer or reader into an intimacy with Indian life through depictions of day-to-day, as well as extraordinary, Indian activities has a way of humanizing Indian people as well. Leigh constructed several of his best Indian paintings around just such intimacy. *Hopi Courtship* (1915), for example, portrays a Hopi couple sitting alone on a stone outcropping, illuminated only by the moon and stars. The woman wears her hair in the traditional Hopi "squash blossom" style, and the man the traditional red headband. They are seemingly musing the idea of marriage without a lot of fuss or overt passion, serene yet thoughtful in the magical night. This couple could be Laughing Boy and Slim Girl, for they are evoked by a poetic simplicity reminiscent of La Farge. In Leigh's *Hopi Firing Pottery* (1912), a similarly simple scene conveys intimacy by showing a Hopi woman on her knees laying the last rocks over a carefully built "kiln" that is traditionally accurate: after creating a bed of hot coals, Indian potters, like the modern Maria Martinez of San Ildefonso Pueblo, balance rocks and pots over the coal bed in precarious combination, and cover the whole over with a framework of dried dung to maintain the smoldering heat. Again, Leigh's attention to such details as dress, hairstyles, and traditional ways emphasizes respect for Indian culture without much undue exoticism.

In *Chende Hogan* (1950), Leigh illustrates the well-known Navajo (and Apache) fear of the dead, also expressed in *Laughing Boy* and in such modern works as Ron Query's *The Death of Bernadette Lefthand* (1993). "Other Indians believe in a similar corpse spirit," writes Matthews, "yet the author has never known any who have such dread as the Navahoes [*sic*] of human mortuary remains."[8] "A dead person was taboo," writes Leigh correctly in his memoirs, "[and] must not be touched. Moreover, the house in which the person died must be destroyed, to the end that the thronging devils might be extirpated."[9]

On the other hand, however, Leigh was not above repeating the Indians-attack-wagon-train syndrome that occupied many western painters and book jacket illustrators. His 1942 painting *Westward Ho* fits into this typical genre, as do several of his cowboy paintings; many other illustrators of the period, struggling to make a living during the war, lapsed into stereotype and convention when they had to. Even Blumenschein, another accomplished and original painter, would illustrate the novels of Zane Grey, an East Coast dentist who wrote cowboy-Indian fantasies with great success. Leigh's *Master of His Domain* (1906–16) shows another unfortunate lapse into conventionality. Against a backdrop that is certainly the desert Southwest, Leigh posed a generic Indian wearing all the accoutrement of a Lakota Sioux (warbonnet, beaded moccasins, parfleche, and medicine bag). Of course, artistic license is not an aesthetic or moral sin, and what constitutes authenticity in art is often more a matter of mood and general effect rather than of photographic realism. Even photographers such as Edward Curtis posed their subjects and dressed them in other than "authentic" ways. Such embellishment is perhaps less forgivable in Curtis, who aspired to an ethnographic record of Indian life in his work.

Leigh's artistic accomplishments, while suffering from an idealization of the Indian as a romantic figure, still show signs of the turning of artistic consciousness away from legendary stereotype to a more socially conscious empathy. Perhaps unaware of the potential political damage to be done to Indians by portraying them in an overly romanticized light, painters of the Southwest such as Leigh were understandably eager to capture the effulgent beauty of the region and its inhabitants, whom many believed were not long for this world. Though their motivation to capture the Indian as a human subject was sincere, even radical individualists like Leigh could not overcome the impress of stereotype, as illustrated in his early uncharacteristic poem "The Painted Desert" (1912).

> *Ah! the lonesome, lonesome places*
> *Of that wan, wide, wasted land,*
> *Where on crazy crooked bases*
> *Giant boulders balanced stand.*
> *Where fantastic spurs and spires,*
> *And titanic mesas rise,*
> *Tinged as by satanic fires*
> *High against cerulean skies.*
> *Carved as by a race of Devils*
> *Who in ultra-freakish moods,*
> *'Mid demoniacal revels,*
> *Sought to mock the solitudes.*

And with drunken reel and laughter,
Splashed crude colors far and wide,
Which kind Nature long thereafter
Touched, and strangely unified.

. . . .

And the wilderness undaunted,
He [the painter] is eager to invade,
And his pathway seems enchanted
And his feet with wings arrayed.
And the mystery and the wonder
Lure him on forever more,
All the lonesome spots to plunder
Of their wealth of secret lore.[10]

Unabashedly romantic, the poem serves to illustrate a white mind-set still obsessed with the deliciously satanic nature of the Indian and the colonial imperative to "plunder / Of their wealth of secret lore."

Two of Leigh's other paintings, *Hopi Indian Runners* (1913) and *A Close Call* (1943), serve to demonstrate how the Indian Other, either as Noble or Ignoble Savage, operates psychologically to validate the need of white culture to fortify itself as the "good." As David Deitcher has noted in his 1991 *New York Times* essay, "A Newer Frontier": "The vast majority of the art in these galleries hinges on a pair of stereotypes [of the Indian]: the 'noble savage,' in harmony with nature, and the bloodthirsty demon, a force of an altogether more malignant nature." Deitcher's observations derive from the controversy surrounding the 1991 National Museum of American Art's exhibition, "The West as America: Reinterpreting Images of the Frontier, 1820–1920," and efforts by the show's curators to demystify much of its content with revisionist (some said "anti-American") rhetoric and compelling new interpretations of the art's significance. "Inventing the Indian" was a major thematic section of the show, and it emphasized the stereotypes that Deitcher mentions and that are still to be seen in some of the pieces at museums of western art throughout the country.

The first painting, *Hopi Indian Runners*, serves as an example of the first, or Noble Savage, stereotype. Three young Indians dominate the foreground of a composition that is expertly romanticized and charismatically painted. Two of the figures are in full stride, closing in on an escaping jackrabbit, while the third has just fallen to the ground, apparently in exhaustion; they appear almost on the surface plane of the canvas, their Olympian bodies caught in a dynamic of taut athleticism, and immediately catch the eye with their exuberance. Oddly, they achieve a double impression of both innocent fun and savage resolve: are they chasing the jackrabbit (who is also turning toward the foreground) for the chaste excitement of the chase, or are the boomerang-like weapons they are hurling at the rabbit meant to kill it? The Hopi did use such weapons to kill prey, and they seem an obvious aboriginal signifier in any case.[11] What further romanticizes the runners is the Turner-esque landscape they are joyously splashing through. What in reality must be the harsh and hot desert of north-central Arizona is rendered by Leigh into atmospherics of pastel lights and soft painterly forms—the desert sand, indeed, seems ethereal enough that only one of the runners is obliged to wear moccasins, the sagebrush seems more like lamb's ear, and there is no hint that this environment can cause great bodily harm if run through unclothed and unshod as depicted.

The faces and heads of the Hopi runners are also strangely rendered—the faces appear leathery, with expressions verging on the grotesque, and the hair is wildly inflamed, suggesting both the motion of the run and an un-tamed psychic nature. In short, they seem exoticized so as to depict a barbar-ian nature, childlike yet cruel. The romantic fascination with exotic races (in this case both genetic and sporting) has its mythological overtones, which as Barthes has observed function to obliterate the responsibility of the artist (and the culture he represents) to depict the life of the Other in realistic, which is to say Native, terms. Applying Barthes's words to Leigh's work:

> The [painting] is euphoric, everything in it is easy, innocent. Our [subjects] are good fellows, who fill up their leisure time with child-like amusements. They play with their mascot [or jackrab-bit]. All this "primitive" folklore whose strangeness seems ostensi-bly pointed out to us has as its sole mission the illustration of "Nature": the rites, the cultural facts, are never related to a par-ticular historical order, an explicit economic or social status, but only to the great neutral forms of cosmic commonplaces. If we are concerned with [Hopi runners], it is not at all the type of [run-ning] which is shown; but rather, drowned in a garish sunset and eternalized, a romantic essence of the [runner].[12]

A Close Call, (oil, 1913) by William R. Leigh, invites speculation as to the nature of the "Other." (From the collection of the Museum of Western Art, Denver, Colorado.)

"All told," Barthes concludes, "exoticism here shows well its fundamental justification, which is to deny any identification with History." *Hopi Indian Runners*, as well, seems a work concocted from romantic ingenuity and exoticism, whose effect, though strikingly beautiful, bespeaks a historical naiveté from which sprang the notion of the Noble Savage.

A Close Call, on the other hand, provides an interesting sidelight on that other stereotype, the flip side of the romantic sublime and its psychological twin—that of the Indian Other as bloodthirsty and savage pagan. While other works of the period show graphic portrayals of Indians massacring, marauding, mutilating, and otherwise threatening white expansionists, this work is haunting in that the enemy is not exactly at hand. In it, a mounted cowboy is seen bursting into the foreground up a rocky escarpment, his gun drawn, his horse terrified, and his hat flying, gaze anxiously turned back over his shoulder. As in the previous painting, the pictorial surroundings are rendered in bright, soft pastels, while the main figures (man and horse) are in an opposing state of vivid coloration and suspended animation. Other than the title's suggestion and the expressions of the rider and horse, however, there is no physical evidence of any threatening aspect, so that what is not portrayed directly becomes suddenly more important to the viewer than what is.

This void is an interesting locus for speculation and for projection, by which viewers are seduced into betraying their own culturally programmed fears. The unknown itself becomes a succinct component of the painting's significance, and a certain psychological dynamic involved in creating the Other comes into play. One is invited to project the stereotype into the painting, rather than have it explicitly drawn out, and in so doing the viewer becomes an active participant in the dynamic of "naming the Other." Was it a rattlesnake the rider encountered? Not likely, considering that whatever it was still poses a threat though it is now at a distance. Was it a rock slide, or a bushwhacker? A mountain lion or marauding bear? Surely the painter would have wanted us to know from whence this excitement comes, were it from something so prosaic as these. No, the *un*-naming of it by the artist seems to imply something more terrifying, more abstract, more spiritually sublime: something more along the lines of the Other, a projection of our innermost fears. In the context of this painting, the marauding Indian's mysterious and fearful Otherness lurks behind the historical moment being depicted, just as it lurks behind the imagery of Leigh's poem above, and behind that of John Ford's film *The Searchers*, where the exact nature of what the "Comanch" have inflicted upon the white women is always left to the imagination of the viewer, though it is always insinuated that the deed was something heinous and probably sexual.[13]

This painting finds its true value, then, in depicting the Other by not depicting it, a tactic through which the Other is seen in its truest sense as a projection of internalized, mythological fear. We need not ever have seen "the devil" to know that he lurks there, waiting to be incarnated by a doctrinal, historical context into a human image.

BERT GEER PHILLIPS

Of the members of the Taos Society of Artists, founded in 1915 as a coopera-tive to negotiate with Simpson, Harvey, the AT&SF Railroad, and the public at large, only three had any demonstrable interest in Indians beyond their usefulness as subjects for painting. While some critics accuse the entire membership of social naiveté, saying that "the imagery they created favored the idyllic and ignored social ills," Bert Phillips, Joseph Sharp, and Walter Ufer all took a personal interest in their Indian subjects and their welfare, though such interest may not always be evident in their paintings.[14] Ernest Blumenschein, a perfectionist and something of a dandy (he has been called a "drugstore cowboy" by historians Sherry Clayton Taggett and Ted Schwarz), was most adept at the business side of the society's relationship with the railroad, negotiating sales, touring exhibitions, and other means of exposing the artists collectively to the public. At Blumenschein's request, Simpson agreed to purchase works for cash money instead of free rail passes and, though the artists received no royalties from the use the railroad made of their paintings afterward (such as postcards, calendars, and prints), they did have a steady market for their work and wide public exposure. Some were commanding $20,000 dollars for a single painting, and demand for the work of all the artists increased dramatically between 1913 and 1927, when the society was dissolved.[15]

Blumenschein, however, epitomized the attitude among early Taos artists that Indians, like the landscape of the Southwest, were incidental to their painting, providing thematic and compositional intrigue essential for painterly romanticizing. While "their images were an affirmation of sympathy with Indian life," argues McLuhan, "these artists were, however, lacking in any apparent awareness of the particularities of the culture they were representing. They painted what they felt and what they wanted to feel."[16] Unlike Phillips, Ufer, and Sharp, Blumenschein had no real interest in particular Indians as people.

Phillips and Blumenschein first entered the Taos Valley in 1898 via buckboard from Denver. Eager to try out anything "western," the two had an arduous trip, plagued by broken wheels and sprung suspensions. Blumenschein walked the last three miles, carrying a wheel into Taos for repair. Once there, it was Phillips who immediately took to the place and its people. He wrote later in his diary, somewhat naively:

> The Indians worship all things beautiful. . . . It is not the passive appreciation that is the frequent reaction to beauty of many white people. It is an integral part of their being. Their religion revolves around the rhythm and life of nature. Their love of beauty is born of knowledge as well as of what we call superstition . . .

Why not expect something unusual from an intelligent people who have had only one book for thousands of years, which they have studied and upon which they have depended for their physical, mental and spiritual life—the book of nature. To understand something of this is to understand something of the Indian people. Their whole life is keyed to the rhythm of nature, as evidenced by their sense of design in their blankets, pottery, baskets and in their music.[17]

Phillips became involved in Taos Pueblo's historic battle over its sacred Blue Lake, becoming the first ranger in the newly created Taos Forest Preserve that oversaw the lake until 1965, when the pueblo finally gained back full title to the 130,000 acres the government had appropriated for the preserve.[18] For his paintings, he would visit Indian friends in their homes instead of posing them artificially in other surroundings, a practice that almost caused him to go blind, due to the lighting conditions under which he painted them there. As a tribute to his real empathy with his Indian friends, some who had posed for him in their homes voluntarily brought props to Phillips's studio, where he had better light.

Phillips's paintings, however, are typical of the genre. *The Last Trail* (n.d.), for instance, portrays an Indian woman getting ready to mount her pony for what is ostensibly a last ride into the sunset, playing on the stereotypical theme of the vanishing breed. *The War Chief* (n.d.) is a rigidly posed portrait of the Noble Savage variety, showing a stolid Indian in a composure of resigned dignity. As Patricia Broder has noted, "Phillips' Indians are not individuals but are representations of an ideal, posed in order to give rhythm and balance to a composition."[19]

That Phillips was somewhat reticent about probing very deeply into Indian life is perhaps best illustrated by his involvement with the Penitente cult of the local Hispanics, whose rather gruesome religious rituals he observed firsthand. Having actually witnessed a human crucifixion, and revolted by both the actual event and the fact that he had jeopardized his own safety by seeing it, he "would be haunted by the spectacle of the Penitentes the rest of his life, a demon he dared not exorcise through art."[20] Instead of painting what might indeed have been a masterpiece of southwestern drama, he chose instead to portray the innocuous and stylized *Penitente Burial Procession*, a dimly lit and distant abstract of a serpentine line of people. Despite his closeness to and good intentions toward Indians, Phillips simply did not have much intimacy with his subjects that could be expressed in his paintings.

JOSEPH SHARP

Joseph Sharp, who first traveled west in 1883, had somewhat better success conveying a sense of Indian vitality and idiosyncrasy in his work. Also sensitive to the plight of Indians,

> he was aware that changes were occurring which would ultimately destroy the various Indian nations as they had existed for centuries. Most Indians were on reservations. Intermarriage among tribes and intermarriage between whites, blacks, or Hispanics and Indians was taking place. The customs, the religion, even the physical appearance of the people would not last.[21]

His concerns carried over into political action as well. In a letter to the Office of Indian Affairs, dated 1902, Sharp responded to the BIA injunction of Commissioner Jones that "[Indian] boys be shorn of their braids and be given haircuts typical of white youths."[22] In the letter, he defended the Indians' right to wear their hair long, pointing out that "it would be the greatest sacrifice you could have them make. . . . [for] only on rare occasions is their grief so great that they cut their hair."[23]

While Phillips had shied away from painting his most visceral experience among the Penitentes, Sharp painted his *Penitente Flagellants* in 1934 based on Phillips's experience. The painting has a dark intrigue that suggests the religious intensity of the local Hispanics who, though not Indians, embody the fervor with which they also practiced their religion. Sharp painted an authentic rendering of Indian ceremonials as well, in *The Harvest Dance of the Pueblo Indians of New Mexico* (1893), which correctly shows dance regalia typical of the Taos people (spruce boughs, gourd rattles, tablitas worn on the head, feather anklets, etc.) and, unlike Leigh's *Navajo Fire Dance*, is noticeably lacking in romantic histrionics. The Indians portrayed do not all look alike, and there is a casual yet reverential communal appeal to the work that seems appropriate. Compared with Blumenschein's highly stylized *Moon, Morning Star, Evening Star* painting of the Taos Deer Dance, Sharp's rendering is much less stylized and exoticized.

Sharp could also paint village life with the same sense of realism. *Taos*

Indians (1924) is composed of six Indians gathered along a bench outside an adobe structure. One smokes a cigarette, and all seem engaged in a casual repartee, dressed in plain blankets (except one) and moccasins. The very lack of decorative embellishment and the unposed look of the subjects contributes to an unusually naturalistic feel, and the subjects are neither glamorized nor degraded, but appear as common folk going about their daily business.

WALTER UFER

Of all the Taos Society painters, Walter Ufer seems the one most attuned to what it meant at the time to be a "real" Indian in a white man's world. Taggett and Schwarz maintain that "Ufer brought the first hint of social consciousness to the area," an assertion that is borne out in some of his paintings.[24] Ufer was a political activist and follower of Trotsky before he arrived in Taos in 1914, and thus well versed in the plight of oppressed

people. As a student in Dresden, he also knew the hard facts of poverty, saving bread crusts in a tin can for those days when he would have nothing else to eat. Once in Taos, he immediately sympathized and identified with the Indians as brothers and sisters of the working classes, people who led exhausting lives just eking out a living. His respect for both the dignity of hard work and the struggle of poverty were not just philosophical: He himself participated in both for most of his life. Although he sold more paintings than most of the other society artists, he was frequently broke and was a hard drinker as well. A volatile, fiercely independent man, Ufer, unlike his contemporaries, resisted the conventional iconography that overlaid most paintings of the Indian, preferring instead to try and picture them on their own terms.

Emphasizing his human kinship with Indians, Ufer painted himself in *Me and Him* (n.d.) as an Indian with an Indian, wearing his hair in identical braids and with each man holding a farming implement—"each man an

Taos Indians (oil, 1924) by Joseph Sharp. (Copyright and reproduction courtesy of the Eiteljorg Museum of American Indians and Western Art, Indianapolis, Indiana.)

equal partner in work."[25] "The Indian is not a fantastic figure," Ufer once told his patron, Chicago Mayor Carter Harrison. "He resents being regarded as a curiosity—as a dingleberry on a tree. He is intelligent and a good businessman . . . and he is quick to challenge any false statements about himself or his life."[26] While most of the other Taos painters posed their figures in alluring, cozy adobes surrounded by traditional Indian crafts and symbolic regalia, Ufer's subjects often appear at work in the service of the white man. *Luncheon at Lone Locust* (n.d.), for instance, shows an Indian waiting tables filled with well-to-do whites, and *Bob Abbott and His Assistant* (n.d.) portrays an Indian man as an apprentice mechanic. In *Jim and His Daughter*, Ufer paints Jim as an "Americanized Indian" wearing cowboy trappings rather than traditional costumery, work clothes that suggest the

Jim and His Daughter, (oil, c. 1915) by Walter Ufer, reflects the artist's empathy with the working-class realities of Indian life. (Courtesy of the National Cowboy Hall of Fame, Oklahoma City, Oklahoma.)

real-life hardships of the Indian cowboy. "In Ufer's paintings," comments Broder, "the contrast of the brilliant sunlit desert with the passive, lifeless figures of the Indians emphasizes the weariness of the Pueblo people and their stoic acceptance of the burdens of life in a transitional age."[27]

Perhaps Ufer's most eloquent and moving statement regarding the post-colonial condition of the Indian is in his painting *Hunger* (n.d.). Before an altar composed of a crucifix, on which hangs a disjointed, doll-like Christ figure, and another reliquary santo common in the Hispanic Southwest, two Indian figures pray in earnest. Christianized Indians, living at the time in a syncretic world in which Christianity, embellished with Native iconography, held sway over traditional Indian ceremonial religions, appeal to the white man's God for relief from their hunger. The painting resonates with the incongruities inherent in the process of assimilation, which Ufer understood was "more in the fantasy of the white man than in reality," and shows Indians as being at cross-purposes with regard to the white man's religion that had simultaneously disenfranchised them and given them surrogate hope for a better life. As Broder observes, "In *Hunger* he utilized the theme of crucifixion and religious images . . . to protest the condition of deprivation and misery in the Indian world."[28] Rather than naively celebrating the beneficence of Christianization, Ufer noted instead the cultural and spiritual dissolution and hunger that it had engendered among his Indian friends.

The era defined by the existence of the Taos Society of Artists is one fraught with contradictions. While Ufer, Phillips, Sharp, Leigh, and the others helped portray Indian people as intelligent, artistic, hardworking, and generally humane, such portrayals were in part the result of the commercial mandates of the new tourist trade. Ufer, for instance, despite his more personally inspired work, "sold a reported $150,000 worth of paintings in three years by turning out the same picture over and over, an Indian on a white horse posed against a Taos mountain looming in the background."[29] Simpson, Harrison, and Harvey, principal among the several significant patrons, were also careful arbiters of what kinds of images of Indians would reach the public, and these were generally "calendar Indians," designed to attract tourists to the Land of Enchantment. Harrison, who had urged Ufer to "consider the realistic presentation of Indians," also insisted that he paint their flesh tone "darker than . . . natural because he feared people would not think they were real Indians."[30] Simpson, writing to Irving Couse about a painting he had submitted for calendar reproduction, advised:

> Note how we [the railroad image makers] have experimented by pasting on a slip to see how it would look if the warbonnet [not a Puebloan feature anyway] was made larger. Rather like the effect, and wish you would kindly correct the sketch accordingly. While the face is attractive and out of the ordinary, [we] . . . feel that it might look a little more like the Indian Chief most of us have in our mind if following changes were made.[31]

Ufer's fear that the Indians had become nothing more than tourist attractions was based on such exploitive and manipulative experiences, of which he himself was obviously guilty as well.

By the same token, the artists themselves wished to protect their vested interest in Indian images. Soon after galleries began publishing price lists of their work, the society put a stop to it, because several Indian models, who were getting twenty-five cents an hour for posing, had read the lists and then insisted on receiving a portion of the going rates. "Instead of being helpful to some nice white men engaged in a rather odd profession, they suddenly saw themselves as valuable parts of a profitable enterprise. They wanted their share."[32]

By 1917, it was too late for the Taos and other Pueblo Indians to effectively stop the white capitalist appropriation of their cultural significance as initiated and perpetuated by the AT&SF. Some, however, would reap the enormous benefits that the tourist trade would bring in the form of an insatiable desire for traditional Indian arts and crafts—a desire that still enriches, albeit not without a great deal of controversy, the lives of many Indian artisans and artists of the Taos–Santa Fe valley. Modern Indian artists, as I will discuss later, are today steeped in controversy over what constitutes Indian art and, indeed, which people within Indian communities are racially eligible to market their art as "Indian." Meanwhile, many Indian and non-Indian artists still rely on the hackneyed images derived from this period for their basic iconography, knowing its long-lasting appeal to those seeking romantic respite from modern American realities.

grounds for mythification 7

FRANK WATERS IN "THE RED ATLANTIS"

Pictorial artists were not the only colonizers of and advocates for the community of Taos. Soon after the founding of the Taos Society of Artists, Mabel Dodge Luhan, a Taos socialite, invited a young Boasian "cultural pluralist" and progressive named John Collier to visit her and tour Taos Pueblo. Collier's reaction to what he witnessed at Taos was soon to have a profound effect on American Indian policy. Kenneth Philp's reiteration of Collier's impression epitomizes the way some white Americans came to adulate certain Indian communities:

> At Taos, Collier discovered that a few hundred Indians "had survived repeated and immense historical shocks" in order to live "amid a context of beauty which suffused all the life of the group." They had created a "Red Atlantis" where community life flourished. Collier believed that his discovery had universal significance because the Indians were the only people in the Western Hemisphere who still possessed "the fundamental secret of human life—the secret of building great personality through the instrumentality of social institutions."[1]

Such were the auspicious theoretical beginnings of the "Indian New Deal," initiated by Collier when he became commissioner of the BIA under Franklin D. Roosevelt, in 1933.

John Collier served for twelve years to reform the Bureau of Indian Affairs and dedicated much of his life to fighting for Indian rights and attracting attention to Indian lifeways as admirable, even enviable, models for human society at large. In his book *On the Gleaming Way*, Collier presents his observations of Indian life among the Navajos, Pueblo Indians, Zunis, Hopis, and Apaches. His disparagement of BIA policies preceding his administration, and of colonizing white society in general, serves to emphasize the way some whites now viewed the "Indian problem":

> An exploitation totally ravenous was practiced by nearly all the white invaders from the first day. Such exploitation breeds hate and scorn toward the victim; and soon the exploiting white soul perceived no longer that garden of marvelous bloom, the Indian spirit in its long summer. Instead, the white man perceived diabolism, benightedness, sloth, bloodthirstiness, and racial impracticability. Secular ruthlessness was supported by religious fanaticism. The destruction of the Indian civilizations came to be an end in itself, and not only a means toward quick wealth; and there was launched the most determined, centuries-long-lasting program of social and spiritual destruction that the world has ever known.[2]

By facing the grim legacy of his office, Collier was able to turn a fresh mind to Indian cultures nationwide, even worldwide, and often found them to be paradigms of enlightened living. He noted the naturalistic practices of the Pueblo Indians, calling them "applied ecologists," and was extremely moved by their "symbol systems," calling their sacred drama "the core of Pueblo life, a personality-forming, an educative institution, possibly without rival in the world of today."[3] He further took a stand against "away schools," noting the ill effects of acculturation as "an all-pervading, undramatic, unconcentrated, ubiquitous peril."[4] He served, in 1926, as a congressional witness to the ceremonies held by the Taos Indians at Blue Lake, often thought to be pagan rituals involving "sadism and obscenity," only to report to the Senate and House Indian Committees that the ceremony was instead "a partnership in an eternal effort whereby, from some remote place of finding and communion, the human and mechanical universes alike are

sustained."[5] He also lobbied Congress throughout the twenties for the reten-
tion of Indian cultural and religious practices, for Indian water, mineral, gas,
and oil rights on reservation lands, and against the Indian Bureau for "[for-
saking] existing programs, broken promises, and establish[ing] new evils."[6]
Collier can perhaps be credited for bringing into the public mind, and that
of several Indian intellectuals, the notions of Pan-Indianism and ethnic
democracy that survive today as viable philosophies geared toward Indian
sovereignty.

Collier's BIA administration offered Indians the promise of the Indian
Reorganization Act (IRA) of 1934, a mixed blessing whereby the tribal
governing bodies of Indian nations were supplanted by tribal councils that
functioned much like state governments under the U.S. Constitution, an-
swerable only to the secretary of the interior or the commissioner. While
Collier recommended that Navajos be privy to the billions of tons of accessi-
ble coal, oil, helium, and other minerals that underlay their reservation land,
ostensibly for their own profit, one of the tragic failures of the IRA is that, to
date, most of the minerals mined on reservations have yielded appreciable
profits only to the non-Indian mining corporations who have leased the
land. Even Collier's heartfelt prescriptions for Indian welfare and his adulation of Indian societies could not stem the greed of neocolonial corporations
and supposed "public interests."

The author of another, less axiomatic, "new deal" for Indians, Frank
Waters settled in Taos in 1938, also introduced to the area (and to the works
of C. G. Jung) by Mabel Dodge Luhan. At the time of his death in 1995,
Waters was ninety-three years old and still had thirteen of his books in print.
Not many of these books receive scholarly attention today, nor have they in
the past, a curious oversight that is only now beginning to be rectified. Too
often, Waters has been dismissed as a regionalist (as if Faulkner and Melville
were not regionalists!) or a "mystic," whose works border on that now ver-
boten literary land of metaphor and magical themes. As David Jongeward
remarks, "His work follows longstanding traditions of writers who have
worked with dream, myth, mysticism, human life rooted in the natural
world."[7] Academic deconstructionists and postmodernists typically resist
literature with such theological presumptions or cosmological underpinnings. But if Barthes is right in suggesting that "the best weapon against
myth is perhaps to mythify it in its turn," perhaps Waters, La Farge, and
others can be forgiven, and even praised, for articulating American Indian

mythology as a linguistic and psychological weapon against white racial stereotypes. In addition, the mythological views of Waters are not unequivocal, nor do they leave us back in the ideological battle over "supreme authority" fought between myth mongers and traditional religions.

Waters was born and raised in Colorado Springs, Colorado, in a marginal neighborhood called Shook's Run. His boyhood, as remembered by his close friend Charles Hathaway, was one of punching bags, pranks, and a sensitivity toward suffering brought out by his grade school exposure to Hugo's *Les Miserables*. His Grandfather Dozier kept a library full of "wonderful books . . . on mysticism or something," some of which Waters apparently read while still an adolescent.[8] He also developed an early empathy with Indians: "I have always, as you know, been interested in Indians," he told Stephen Kress for *Hoka Hey Magazine* in 1992. He himself was alleged to be of "one-tenth" Cheyenne blood, though he is generally referred to as an "Anglo" by Indian purists. In any case, Waters had, since 1930, been writing extensively of Indians, Hispanics, and Anglos of the American Southwest in ways that are largely atypical and in great empathy with his Native subjects. In so doing, he finally earned the praise of a wide spectrum of Indian activists, intellectuals, and writers (such as Vine Deloria Jr. and Leslie Marmon Silko), white academics (such as Charles Adams, Quay Grigg, and Alexander Blackburn), and other southwestern writers and scholars (such as Rudolfo Anaya, Win Blevins, and David Jongeward).

For purposes of this discussion, I have selected three of Waters's works as illustrative of his experiential as well as mythopoetic literary adventures among the Pueblo Indians of New Mexico and Arizona. *The Book of the Hopi*, published in 1963 by Swallow Press, then of Denver, is a uniquely antianthropological work, composed from interviews with "sixty or seventy" Hopi elders who voluntarily offered Waters and his Hopi interpreter, Oswald White Bear Fredericks, a broad pastiche of Hopi creation stories, legends, ceremonial practices, cosmology, and cultural anecdotes that serve to illuminate Indianness from a spiritual as well as historical point of view, through Indian eyes. In conjunction with this book, *Pumpkin Seed Point* is the autobiographical account of the three years Waters spent among the Hopi, interviewing and translating *The Book of the Hopi*. *Pumpkin Seed Point* brings to light Waters's intense identification with Indian lifeways and philosophy, an identification that belies stereotypical notions of the potential relationship between white and Indian cultures, despite the resentment that some Hopis hold against Waters today. It also contains his analysis of how Indians and whites have dehumanized and scapegoated each other—an analysis that reflects the major concerns of this discussion.

The Man Who Killed the Deer represents Waters's most successful attempt to portray the Indian fictionally as a viable and unromanticized human entity, replete with a recognizable psychological reality, motivation, emotional content, complex personality, bodily awareness, social consciousness, and wry humor. Taken together, these three works exemplify a linguistic and psychological impetus against stereotypes and racial ideology that forms and informs the modern search for the "real" Indian. They serve the Indian cause through their sense of humanness, their descriptive power, and immense respect for things Indian. They are firsthand accounts, observations, and extrapolations that defy Otherness as it has traditionally been applied to Native Americans. Beyond these attributes, they are also examples of a literary style that can indeed be revolutionary in its honesty and attention to the prelinguistic provocations for language, with all their psychological ramifications.

THE BOOK OF THE HOPI

> The religious leader of the Taos Pueblo, known as the Loco Tenente Gobernador, once said to me: "The Americans should stop meddling with our religion, for when it dies and we can no longer help the sun our Father to cross the sky, the Americans and the whole earth will learn something in ten years' time, for then the sun won't rise anymore." In other words, night will fall, the light of consciousness is extinguished, and the dark sea of the unconscious breaks in.
>
> C. G. Jung, The Archetypes and the Collective Unconscious

The Book of the Hopi, like *Masked Gods* and *Mexico Mystique*, also by Waters, is a major ethnological and mythological work that divulges background material for some of his novels as well as informs us of the origins of Waters's own metaphorical underpinnings and grand thematic tropes. His interest in the socializing and psychotropic forces at play in aboriginal cultures, whether of the Hopi, the Navajo, or the Nahuatl-speaking peoples of Mexico, also seems crucial for the way he formulates his underlying fictional themes. From these forces Waters also derives something of a mythic authenticity or, as deconstructionists would have it, a guarantee of the spiritual authority of his work. For Waters's work tends toward the bildungsroman in general intent and his fiction, like his mythological studies, commonly propounds a metaphysics that interacts with social reality in such a way as to become something of a catechism or instructional technique in the ethics of living. As for Collier and the Taos artists, Puebloan culture seems also for Waters a socioreligious paradigm worthy of emulation and articulation.

The Hopi culture of the Southwest, centered for centuries around the Three Mesas area east of the Grand Canyon in Arizona, remains one of the most unique and self-contained Indian cultures. Calling themselves the *Hopituh*, or "peaceful ones," the Hopi have been one of the most protected and protective of the Pueblo tribes. Even in Coronado's day, the Hopi managed to thwart intrusion into their homeland. Waters's *The Book of the Hopi* is largely made up of firsthand accounts of tribal elders who, after centuries of secrecy and distrust of the power of the printed word (and of that "Word" that brought the white man to their door), reveal to Waters and his Hopi "recorder," Oswald White Bear Fredericks, what Waters calls their "world-view of life, deeply religious in nature, whose esoteric meaning they have kept inviolate for generations uncounted."[9] Within this revelation, Waters finds important contrasts between Hopi beliefs and the conquering racism and rationalism of white Europeans, and he consistently brings these to the foreground of the discussion.

Although Waters does his best not to romanticize the Hopi position, the ages-old conflict between rational materialism and subjective spiritualism is the central and tragic theme of the work. But it is to Waters's credit that he avoids painting the Hopi as Rousseauian Noble Savages and merely uses their basic tenets to affirm that they may indeed "have a depth psychology different from our own," and that we might learn a lesson from them by way of balancing our Western dissociative neuroses with a dose of natural law and a recognition of the unconscious creative forces that form it, in the Hopi (and Jungian) view.[10] It may also be said that Waters rarely condescends to the Hopi as if they were primitives or savages, but rather sees them as extraordinarily enlightened people. Like some postmodernist critics, Waters detests the premise of ethnology that forces it to murder that which it studies by relegating it to the position of the Other.

The book is an eloquent song of origins; the myths, legends, and their ceremonial reenactments are strung together into a comprehensive whole. The origin myth itself, like others worldwide, begins with the "Void" and the creation of the first world. However, God is notably not the "Father" but the "Uncle" of his first creation, indicative of the matrilineal nature of Hopi society, and the first words spoken are: "Why am I here? Who are we?"— certainly not questions asked by innocents in a patriarchal Eden, but rather by those seeking identity. There is a primary emphasis placed on sound and "vibration" as psychic connections with the Creator—"the universe quivered in tune."[11] The first humans are made with four colors of clay (for fundamental racial tolerance), and the spectral changes of the Sun represent the emotional development of the human race. Typically, evil is also cast into the world: The first sin as promoted by Lavaihoya, "the Talker," is racial and ethnic intolerance—the awareness of differences—that precedes the stigmatization of the Other. As Charles Adams has noted, "To the Hopi, the ultimate evil is . . . the illusion of separateness."[12] The second sin is sexual perversion and warlike aggression; the third sin, avarice and materialism. The earth is destroyed three times because of these sins, and each time it is re-created a little less perfect than the time before: "the way becomes harder and longer."[13]

Waters, with a prior knowledge of Tibetan Buddhism gained by his long association with Buddhist scholar W. Y. Evans-Wentz, notes appropriately the marked similarities between the Hopi version of "psycho-physical centers in the human body" and that of the "cakras" of Tibetan mysticism.[14] He also notes the occurrence of the Cretan symbol of the labyrinth of Daedalus in Hopi culture, as the symbol of "Emergence" or spiritual rebirth. In his closing commentary on "the myths," Waters stresses the psychic as well as the physical connections between the Hopi and Eastern mystical religions, sounding a theme that recurs in his fiction and his personal essays: the future revelation of the mystical unity of humankind.[15]

Hopi life as it is still lived in their Three Mesas homeland is replete with the animistic mysteries associated with nature religions the world over. Daily life is constantly poised between the natural and the supernatural, the two being somewhat indistinguishable in the "primitive" consciousness. As Victor Turner has surmised concerning the hunting and gathering tribes of Africa, "the borderline between the concrete and the symbolic was blurred: [they] could not separate the natural from the supernatural."[16] Hopi culture, like most Native cultures, is rife with symbolism that links human beings with the creation metaphorically, and with complex, ritualistic ceremonies that confirm that relationship perennially. Corn, for instance, takes on several symbolic permutations as the transubstantiating food of life, the staff of life; as "the sacred entity embodying the male and female elements"; as the Corn Mother who provides spiritual nourishment and is "fastened to the sacred mongko—the 'law of laws' "; and, as cornmeal, the Road of Life spread out before the people.[17] Religious societies and clans apply the traditional symbolism during what Waters calls "The Mystery Plays": "the annual cycle of nine great religious ceremonies that dramatize the universal laws of life."[18]

Waters details the enactment of the nine ceremonies with unabashed reverence, making them read, indeed, like the Christian Mystery Plays. During The Night of the Washing of the Hair, for instance, "pairs of Two Horns and One Horns" (two of several "kiva clans") close off all roads to the village except one, and,

> Hearing a step or glimpsing a passing shape, they call out loudly "Haqumi? Who are you?" Immediately the answer comes back, "Pinú'u, I am I," revealing that the accosted one is one of the spiritual beings who has come by way of the one open trail.[19]

Waters's attraction to the mysticism and natural beauty of the Hopi worldview and its attendant rituals and myths resembles that of W. B. Yeats to the ancient Celtic legends or that of William Blake to Druid culture—each of them constructing a personal metaphorical framework and mythology around the prehistoric ones. Regarding the Hopi, however, Waters has the further advantage of being able to interact with this still vital archaic paradigm and to witness its "presence" firsthand and in conflict with modern civilization.

THE MAN WHO KILLED THE DEER

In *The Man Who Killed the Deer*, Waters has created a story of the poignant, lingering tensions that exist between the culture of the Taos Pueblo Indians and that of their two imperial neighbors in the Southwest of the 1930s. The same rhythmic, somnambulant mysticism evident in *The Book of the Hopi* comes to life in this tale of a young Indian, Martiniano, who must face the contradictions of his unique historical position as an "away school" Indian who returns to "the blanket" after an inner quest for faith leads him back to his tribal roots. The guiding literary principle of the work is the reunion of the natural and the supernatural, the mundane and the mythic, and the literal and the metaphorical in the psyche of Martiniano, restoring him to an identity that is in harmony with his personal and cultural history.

Because he has lost the tribal way, Martiniano kills a deer without asking for its permission, a violation of the ethical code of his people. As Underhill notes, this is not a fictional contrivance, but an ongoing ethic among most hunting tribes, where wildlife is seen as having a preeminent and beneficent relationship with human life: "the hunter practiced a form of conservation that was part religious and part practical."[20] Having been caught in the act of poaching as well, he is beaten by forest rangers and lies injured, near death, until his silent cries are "heard" psychically by his friend Palemon, asleep in his *casita*. Palemon rescues him, and the story of Martiniano's partial reintegration into tribal ways plays out in a fascinating concatenation of events and visions through which Waters evokes the archetypal connections between Martiniano and his innate Indianness, an Indianness that he has partially forfeited in his experience at the BIA boarding school.

There are distinct historical resonances that contribute to the tension of the story and lend authenticity to Waters's portrayal of his Indian characters. In 1906, Theodore Roosevelt proclaimed 130,000 acres of the most sacred Taos Indian land a public forest reserve. Within that reserve was the aforementioned Blue Lake, the site of ancient and abiding religious ceremonials and a central symbol in Taos spiritual life, and over which painter Bert Phillips became the first forest ranger. The pueblo's sixty-year fight to regain title to Blue Lake plays a contextual role in the novel as an example of Indian political acuity and persistence, standing in marked contrast to the BIA stereotype of "incompetent Indians" unable to maintain stewardship of their land. Additionally, the historical formation of the Native American Church and its attendant religious use of peyote is included as a subplot, as Martiniano joins the church hoping to facilitate his retribalization. Through his use of such historical referents, Waters places readers squarely in the middle of the "Indian problem" so they may experience it directly and thus become aware of the Indian's historical vulnerability and responsible creativity. As Quay Grigg says of Waters's Indian characters,

> People in his great series of books into the 1940s have a "collective" quality that replaces the self more traditional characters were made of, but they go beyond the usual stereotypes and myths. One way they go beyond stereotypes is in their timelessness, or their encompassing elements of the past as well as the present. . . . They might be called archetypes with deep imprint of the place and culture they derive from.[21]

Indeed, both Waters and La Farge have imbued their characters with a highly effective admixture of spiritual profundity and personal banality, of nature and supranature, so as to create personalities of deep and paradoxical interest. They seem to possess a literary strength that carries them into the ambiguous realm of archetypes. In part, this is accomplished through the sheer craft of writing "the things" instead of writing about them, to paraphrase Barthes. "It is rather Waters' language, itself the pulse," writes Win Blevins, "making us experience his central idea rather than think about it."[22]

Waters achieves a certain syncretic victory in his manipulation of the main trope of "the deer," which comes progressively to embody both the mythic relationship between nature and humankind and the transitive linguistic relationship between literal events and their symbolic significance. Combining a keen sense of realistic style and natural observation with a conviction that unseen forces lie behind human events, which he imparts with laudable romantic ingenuity, Waters elucidates both sociopolitical drama and the enantiodromian (drama of opposites), endopsychic revelations of individuals in conflict with themselves and their society. The result is a multilayered, multivoiced tableau that manages to offer both an epiphany of romantic vision and the poignancy of its displacement by the "necessities" of historical materialism. But most of all, the novel is about the perennial "presence" of the Indian as an archetypal reality.

If the power of literary vision can indeed contribute to the political construction of the world, then I am inclined to view *The Man Who Killed the Deer* as a premier example of the kind of writing that, like a humble prophet, does its work and then recedes back into the mystery of life. The character of Rodolfo Byers, for instance, a white trader who befriends Martiniano and seems a party to the omniscient, third-person voice in the book, is described as "a man who in his immense solitude was something of all men, and of the wilderness around him."[23] He is also the recipient of a strange dream in which an unknown man flashes a powerful word to him that he knows he must always remember "as a talisman," but the "word itself was lost." Furthermore, "it was the substance of life he loved, not form."[24] If this strange white trader Byers can be taken as an alter ego of the writer, we can perhaps see within him an ethic of writing that promotes the word as a functioning sign pertaining to the making of the world, which is then "lost," in that it disappears after its work is done. A principal concern of Barthes—that language not take on the momentum of "pseudophysis" or metalanguage that perpetuates myth and stereotype—seems also that of Waters the writer: not to contaminate the primal stage of Indian life with literary forms that, like a purloined romanticism or an ethnology, tend to freeze-dry palpable reality into a scripted myth.

Waters also uses Byers to debunk Noble Savage stereotypes of the Indian:

> He [Byers] knew their surface indolence and cunning, their dirt and filth and lice, their secretiveness, barbarity, ignorance and stubborn denial of change. And so no man could better refute the sickly sentimentalism of lady tourists, the pampering enthusiasm of museum collectors, the false idealism of escapists and the mock gravity of anthropologists, ethnologists and myth mongers toward them—all the whining, shouting voices that proclaimed the Indian as nature's pet, a darling of the gods, and the only true American.[25]

This kind of self-effacement from a mixed-blood and avowed "friend of the Indian" becomes indicative of Waters's attempts to keep his prose productive of a reality, not reproductive of it ad infinitum as mythical stereotype. He attempts to invoke a writing style that comes close to that language most associated with the Indian, that of sign language, which he praises as "the expressive free-flowing gestures of dark, poetic hands that will always remain, unforgotten, the most expressive medium of their wordless souls."[26] Because Indian cultures are based on an oral and gestural tradition, not a written one, this attention to prelinguistic expression reminds the reader that linguistically constructed stereotypes do not ascend into humanness, and that archetypes, when constellated as reflections of personality or culture, can best render the facts of human complexity.

Furthermore, as Barthes recommends in his pronouncements on poetry, a curious "tangible analogue of silence" seems to linger behind Waters's style; the words seem at times to coalesce into a moment of that silent experience of the archaic or presemiological mind or, as Barthes puts it, they form, like poetry, a "semiological system which has the pretension of contracting into an essential system."[27] Several of Waters's descriptions of the environment inside the ceremonial kiva move toward this kind of contraction:

> The kiva, each kiva, was now itself a vibrating drum. A single star visible through the aperture at the top quivered as if painted on the vibrous, skin-tight membrane of the sky stretched overhead. In the middle of the round floor, like a dot within a circle, was

another symbol—a little round hole, the opening to the center of the world, the place of emergence. The circular walls quivered.[28]

There is a hypnotic, psychotropic effect from this passage that is the result of its careful imagery. A "vibrating drum," "a single star," the metamorphosis of the drum into the "membrane of the sky," "a dot within a circle"—all combine to lead the reader's mind into a focal trance that seems full of the silence of "wordless souls." One is reminded of the similarly haunting lines of Emily Dickinson's poem #216:

> Grand go the Years—in the Crescent—above them—
> Worlds scoop their Arcs—
> And Firmaments—row—
> Diadems—drop—and Doges—surrender—
> Soundless as dots—on a Disc of Snow—[29]

Neither passage produces any sound, color, or smell, and both are notable for their common invocation of silent, mythopoetic intrigue.

Waters's interest in this silence is articulated throughout the novel:

> And when the guttural Indian voice finally stops there is silence. A silence so heavy and profound that it squashes the kernel of truth out of his words, and leaves the meaningless husks mercilessly exposed. . . . And the silence grows round the walls, handed from one to another, until all the silence is one silence, and that silence has the meaning of all.[30]

Or,

> so exquisite was the feeling that possessed [Martiniano]. The yellow moon low over the desert, the stars twinkling above the tips of the high ridge pines, the fireflies, the far-off throb of a drum, the silence, the tragic, soundless rushing of the great world through time—it caught at his breath, his heart.[31]

The effect of this silence is to draw the reader into the real stage of the story and its "essential system," that being the ostensible Puebloan Indian worldview in all its mystery, and the premise that "life is like the surface of a deep blue lake into which a stone is cast."[32]

It also represents an effort on the part of the author to control his significations and to keep his metaphors close to their natural cause in the interest of his theme, that of uniting Martiniano with his own primal silence. Martiniano, filled with the discursive ego reality that has been injected into him at "away school," and experienced by him as "jangling human vibrations," is at first the "Americanized Indian." Through his successive experiences with the vibratory world of Indian awareness, this colonized mind-set, troubled by linguistic and psychological interventions that betray his Indianness, slowly give way to the silence of the kiva. The language of silence serves the theme, as Grigg explains, in that,

> losing his own voice, Martiniano has achieved the stillness and the silence to become part of the collective voice of the pueblo stream of consciousness. He "moves together"—with the pueblo, with the life-force, and with the parts of himself he had suppressed. The novel itself has flowed altogether: the image of the stone thrown into the lake, producing in its successive circles a diagram of sound waves, has merged with the motif of the [kiva] of silence.[33]

"Inside that framework, Waters has moved through and beyond the stereotypes of the taciturn Indian and the picturesque native ceremonials."[34]

As Baudrillard says regarding the "successive phases of the image": in the first phase, closest to a "basic reality," "the representation is on the order of sacrament."[35] Father Peter J. Powell concurs, saying that Waters's work "display[s], with singular power, a uniquely consistent witness to the presence of the Holy in both the Native Peoples and the land of America."[36]

Does Waters verge on mystification, or does he wisely restrain himself from, in Paul de Man's words, "the error of identifying what cannot be identified"?[37] Does the effect of silence merely conceal an effort by the author to guarantee a spiritual presence, the old gods of the Puebloan culture, which in turn guarantees the meaning and authenticity of his story? Obviously, the religious and mystical bent of the author becomes something of a semiological point from which we could embark on a deconstructive assessment of his work. We may be skeptical of such of Waters's assumptions as: "The instinctive, intuitive, non-reasoning approach to life; the magnificent surrender of self to those unseen forces whose instruments we are, and the fulfillment of whose purposes gives us our only meaning," or "Who doubts the great magnetic currents of the earth, or the psychic radiations of man?"[38] But skepticism is not criticism, nor should whole periods and genres of literature be dismissed because they contain "religious" belief and "greater-than-human" metaphors of one sort or another. Given texts of this kind, the deconstructionist critic is left merely to demonstrate his Nietzschean sophistication and his "courage" in demystification. It seems more productive to approach the work of Frank Waters with a tentative acceptance of his assumptions and to proceed to see how they function through the fictional lives of his work as a human and literary force.

Waters himself realizes this tension between the rational and the nonrational, the natural and the supernatural, and the various determining characteristics of each, in the person of his hero, Martiniano, whose crisis of faith is parallel to that crisis in criticism between the hermeneutics of restoration and the hermeneutics of suspicion; and if it is Waters's choice to have his hero at least partially restored to the traditional spiritual identity of his tribe, then that seems his authorial right. The choice that some deconstructionist critics ask us, as readers, to make regarding the metaphorical underpinnings of a given text is akin to Martiniano's choice to accept or reject the spiritual authenticity of his people. Indeed, it is not a wholly unequivocal choice: Martiniano still retains his autonomy and his uncertainty, knowing in the end that "there was no road, predetermined and secure, that he could lay for his son. There was only the faith that his life was the courage of man to make his own step in darkness, his single glimmer, and pass on unafraid."[39] Thus it seems, in context, that nothing is being "protected" or essentialized in the text, and that its power rests on an affirmation of human difference, archetypal ambiguity, and an analogue of prelinguistic silence.

In *The Man Who Killed the Deer*, Waters demonstrates by his concern for historical reality, his willingness to create Indian characters who appear as complex human beings, and his uniquely evocative writing style, that he is aware of the accrued stereotypes of the Indian and their degrading effects upon real Indians through time. In their place, he has created recognizably human Indian subjects, faced with the accumulating problems of assimilation, conversion, the reservation bureaucracy, tribal and personal identity, land grabbing, alcoholism, and poverty, among others, while still retaining a distinct Indianness, however inchoate that term might be. One comes away from the novel with a feeling of reverence for all life, of which the Indian emerges as the predominant witness. "Is Indian humanness recognized?" asks Stedman, citing his own criteria for recognizing stereotypes:

Perhaps this is the only question that need be asked when looking at the Indian of popular culture, for when people are seen as people, conscious or unconscious slights tend to disappear. The anonymous "they" are far more vulnerable to suspicion or prejudicial treatment than are groups recognized as being composed of individuals—even if those individuals are characters of fiction.[40]

Regarding these works by Waters, La Farge, and even Jackson, the issue of humanness as a basic ingredient of fictional Indian identity seems readily at hand, determined in large part by the way each character constellates the archetypal influences that erupt in his or her being.

PUMPKIN SEED POINT

While Frank Waters generally eschews the more objective approaches to Indian life of anthropology and ethnology, preferring instead to experience their cultures subjectively and personally, his experiences nonetheless usually culminate in his writing as philosophical pronouncements no less didactic than scientific theory. Waters spent most of his last fifty years living in daily contact with the Indians of the Taos Pueblo or those of other Pueblo tribes in New Mexico and Arizona, and he cultivated a casual and purposeful intimacy with them that belies the stereotypical notions imparted by some government researchers, statisticians, and BIA policymakers. Somewhat in the ethnological spirit of Franz Boas's "cultural relativism," which stressed "cultural holism and pluralism," Waters has tried to understand Indian cultures on their own terms as unified and significant social systems consisting of individuals as they exist in present contexts. He has recognized that different tribes have different socializing precepts, and that individuals within each tribe are different from others within the same tribe. For Waters, Indians are not "all alike," though they often share common cultural and personality traits, linguistic heritages, and cosmological beliefs. He is just as likely to render an individual Indian as a unique, idiosyncratic personality as he is to draw from his cumulative experience among many Indians a universal, paradigmatic overview of their commonality. "In the process," believes Vine Deloria Jr., "we are very gently nudged in the direction of Frank's own personal question that seeks to know the nature, content, and structure of reality—what is it that is real?"[41] That Waters seeks to know "reality" through his experiences with Indian lifeways and individuals is sufficiently evident in *Pumpkin Seed Point*, a recollection of his three years spent among the Hopi of New Oraibi, Arizona, while collecting the information published in *The Book of the Hopi*. It is also reflective of his honest intent to find the reality behind Indianness, to break down white-written stereotypes, and to exalt humanness in his conception and experience of Indian identities.

This humanness, of course, cannot emerge in literature or in life without the abandonment of both the major stereotypes of Noble and Ignoble Savage and their attendant subtypes. Waters's experiences at Pumpkin Seed Point certainly belie both the nostalgia of primitivism and the epiphanic hope of millenarianism that tends toward prophecy in some of his work. The actual physical conditions of his stay at New Oraibi hardly romanticize primitivism. He is housed in a small, old stone house plastered over with adobe, a typical Hopi structure lacking central heating, plumbing, and electricity, and even lacking a fireplace to keep off the chilling cold. "The Hopis couldn't afford fireplaces, and they conserved every splinter of wood to burn in their cooking stoves." Neither is the rest of New Oraibi an idyllic setting: "Tawdry villages they were, their crooked streets and cramped plazas littered with refuse and ordure."[42] Because the Hopi are among the few Indian tribes who were not driven off their ancestral land, and have indeed inhabited the same locale fairly undisturbed by white and Spanish influences since the fourteenth century, it is assumed, and has been historically verified, that they live today in much the same fashion as they did then. For the Hopi, there is no romantic past to connect them with a yesteryear utopia. "Of all the Indian tribes in North America, the Hopis probably live closest to their traditional way," a way made obdurate and desolate by its physical realities, locale, and economics.[43] They are also one of the very few tribes not to have adopted Christian symbolism and iconography into their ceremonial life, although Collier bemoans the effects of the Mennonite Church under H. R. Voth on Hopi lifeways in his *On the Gleaming Way*.[44]

Witnessing such bleak environs, a typical white writer such as Mark Twain might infer that its inhabitants too are primitive, unwashed, ignorant, and dispossessed of any cultural significance. Waters finds quite the opposite among the Hopis he meets during his tenure there. His associate and interpreter is Oswald White Bear Fredericks, with whom he shares all his meals and leisure time as well as work on the project. Fredericks's white wife, Brown Bear (her adopted Hopi name), is also a coworker and friend. Although Fredericks has converted to Christianity, he also stands in line to become a Hopi religious leader as a member of the Bear Clan.

Typical of the away-school Indian, Fredericks was sent as a boy to Indian School in Phoenix and two other bureau schools before returning with his white wife to Hopiland. Waters is very keen to recount what he knows of Fredericks's history and his personality, in a way that can only be called affectionate. Neither condescending nor overly critical, Waters accepts "the two Bears" as his "closest friends in New Oraibi," and they emerge for the reader as fully rounded personalities.[45] White Bear is recalcitrant yet enthusiastic, obdurate yet humble and devout, both a prophet of his people and a powerless political force. Brown Bear is irascible, a "wannabe" Indian who has a hard time adjusting to reservation life, yet a tireless hostess, cook, and typist. In short, they are both quirky, idiosyncratic individuals full of paradoxical human charm.

Whether Waters is describing Old Dan the medicine man or Otto Pentiwa, the town trickster and storyteller, the characters are drawn complete with history, personality, and affection. They are not just human characters, but also actors in the "living faith" of Hopi ceremonialism: "The flower grown from Hopi poverty and dirt was the kachina, an art form unequaled anywhere else in the world; a flower of faith such as we have not been able to grown out of our antiseptic culture pot."[46] Kachinas, expressive of the multitudinous divinities who inform Hopi culture, appear as masked dancers and actors during the great ceremonials, impersonated by "each man in his turn," according to his clan affiliations. They are the essence of Hopi myth and religion, and exist as both esoteric "star people," who come to the pueblos from deep interstellar space, and as exoteric masked men who, after a day in the fields or herding sheep, become ritually transformed into the archetypal gods and goddesses of Hopi mythology. Such is the fecund paradox of Puebloan culture and the essence of its humanity, "that out of a garbage heap, a pile of manure, often grows the most beautiful flower."[47] As Collier similarly observed of the Navajo, "How can so rich a flower bloom in a soil so rocky and nearly waterless?"[48]

While such panegyrics might suggest a mythifying romanticism, Waters's ambivalence toward the Hopi way, like La Farge's toward the Navajo way, steers the naive reader away from the cloying notion of the mystical warrior or Noble Savage. His unabashed reverence for the sacramental nature of Hopi life merely emphasizes his acceptance of the complex archetypal nature of "real" Indianness and the resulting cultural sophistication that such symbolic relationships with the world imply. For stereotypes to dissolve, the "basic reality" suggested by Baudrillard as containing the sacramental must be recovered as an archetypal image, and Waters achieves this end, both here and in *The Book of the Hopi, Masked Gods*, and *Mexico Mystique*. The stereotype of the Indian as devoid of any cultural significance, as a heathenish primitive who understands "spirits" only as whiskey, as Twain remarked, gives way under the careful scrutiny of Waters to real people taking part in a living cosmology, whose archetypal figures come to dance nine times every year at Puebloan ceremonials, in a living dramaturgy that loves the men behind the masks as much as their symbolic resonance. "At supreme moments, [Waters's characters] seem to be the kachina; more often, they are more like the masked impersonators of kachinas."[49]

It seems crucial that white Christians, who have inherited the imbedded stereotypes of the Indian imagined by their forefathers, be enjoined to understand that the Indian possesses a spiritual capacity as profound as any alleged within the Christian mythos. Surely we cannot say without prejudice that the supernaturalism inherent in the risen Christ or his communion of transubstantiation is more or less mystical, or more or less acceptable to reason, than the Hopi belief that the kachinas "are intermediaries between the Creator and humankind." They, like Christ, explains Lamson Lowatemama, a Hopi educator and poet, "deliver the blessings of life—health and happiness and hope."[50] For Waters to bring Hopi cosmology and myth into the mind of the "master race" is to expose the common spirituality among human beings that enables and provokes them to engender myths of whatever form. But that any particular mythical form should be declared the "single principle" under which all humanity must labor is to comply with colonial tyranny and to ignore the immense diversity of spiritual expression that pervades the world. As Mircea Eliade notes, "only the forms taken by the process in man's religious consciousness differ"; their significance to the humanness of any race or culture does not.[51] "I discovered," remembers Waters,

> that every Hopi in some measure, like myself, was two persons: an
> outer man consciously confronted with the problems of existence
> in a swiftly changing, material world; and an inner man attuned
> to the greater realm of the unconscious, the matrix of all cre-
> ation. . . . I lay in bed after work each night scribbling notes . . .
> and anecdotes about the Hopis who projected their fears and
> prejudices on the whites who for so long have projected their own

fears and prejudices on all Indians. Two invisible projections clashing in the air.[52]

Waters, like Frantz Fanon, realizes the spectral nature of projection, as it artificially engenders racial ideologies abetted by the imperatives of clashing myths.

Does Waters wish us to abandon Christianity in preference for Hopi mythology? Does he indeed believe that any myth, no matter how sublime, beautiful, or consistent with natural law, should become predominant as a millenarian prophecy or a paradigmatic dogma? His feelings about the compulsive secrecy and exclusivity of Hopi religious leaders seem to indicate that he does not. Although he respects the sanctity of Hopi religion as "spiritual property . . . not to be given away lightly," he also voices a tactical resistance to it on the grounds that it, like Christianity, functions mainly to promote "fears and prejudices" between races and the perpetuation of stereotypes:

> Beneath their kind and placid demeanors . . . I began to detect in all their talks an embittered condemnation of the white world's dominating injustices, alternating with unqualified assertions that Hopi ritualism contained the exclusive secret of universal life. . . . It is so easy for us, as well as the Hopis, to blame all our misfortunes and defects on others; to nurse in secret the superior sanction which makes us different from the rest of mankind. Yet it is exactly this which fatally exiles an individual, or a nation, from others, depriving him of the healing communion with the whole society of man. It is the sign of a messianic compulsion of an individual, or a race, possessed by the mythology of an inherent superiority.[53]

Certainly Waters's exposure here of the crucial association between scapegoating, projection, messianic compulsion, race, and mythology reveals a larger interest in demythologizing human consciousness. Because myth relies on the distillation of diversity into essential types, myth itself cannot but perpetuate these types as surrogate realities without history or individual character. Waters's ambivalence toward Hopi myth, and indeed all myth, thus allows him to both eulogize it as a humanizing force that delineates "real" Indians as sacramental and culturally autonomous and, simultaneously, to detect in it "the obverse and negative side of the great structure of

Hopi ceremonialism."[54] Barthes, reflecting on the tendency of myth to present the world as a "harmonious display of essences," notes that "a conjuring trick has taken place."[55] "The essence of witchery," echoes Waters, "is the projection of the repressed dark forces of the unconscious by one individual or people upon another."[56]

In his chapter "The Evil Eye," Waters elaborates on this point with great success. Like other scholars who note the obvious corollaries between Euramerican racial ideology and that of the German Nazis, Waters provides a telling analogy based on the ideas of witch-hunting and projection.[57] Arguing that Nazism represents a resurgence of long-suppressed "demonic forces under Thor and Wotan rushing toward another Gotterdammerung," Waters suggests that Hitler, possessed by the "dark luciferean shadow" of his Teutonic heritage, gained credence through the power of witchcraft conceived as projection:

> All four of the Nazi leaders dressed in Teutonic armor when they met in secret sessions. These meetings were actually Sabbats of witches, for Hitler, Hess, Goebbels, and Haushofer were quite aware of the technique of psychological projection. And all Germany welcomed the domination of its warlock leaders.[58]

Similarly, some of our Puritan forefathers, convinced that they were involved in an ancient battle between God and Satan, projected their own dark side on the Indian and other "miscreants," such as the "witches" who were burned in Salem in 1692. As I have noted earlier, the Jungian concept of projection is at the root of several modern interpretations of the psychological and semiological dynamics of myth making and racial ideology, from that of Jung himself to those of Frantz Fanon, Barthes, Baudrillard, Berkhofer, and now Waters. "Our own almost complete extermination of the red race under the national witch-hunt slogan, 'The only good Indian is a dead Indian,' has left us a hangover worse than our original drunkenness, a psychotic prejudice against all races of darker skin."[59] From the legacy of the BIA to our present-day Indian policy, the disfiguring stereotypes of the Indian have been the imagistic constellation of these projections, further distorted by the uncertainty of their real origins. The Ignoble Savage clears the way for colonial expansion, conversion, and extermination. The Noble Savage clears the way for assimilation, appropriation, and spiritual poverty.

2

From Stereotype to Archetype

from western art to archetype 8

THE PATH OF THE SPIRIT IN MODERN INDIAN ART

Forces in corporate and political America insist that all Americans in the 1990s
share identical goals, desires, and dreams—that they aspire to be rich, white,
blonde—and frenetic consumers. Americans in general do not mold to these
insults; American Indians do not, either. Both, as Americans are prone to do,
constantly reinvent themselves.

Stephen Trimble

TRADITION . . . in painting, music, religion, and other human consciousness is
only as good as the lasting shock presented when it was a ruthless vanguard sin
of the times.

T. C. Cannon, Kiowa-Caddo artist

Heretofore we have been concerned with the construction and proliferation
of Indian stereotypes and archetypes created largely by white writers and
artists, from the policymakers and bureaucrats of the BIA to the hailed
filmmakers of Hollywood and the more sensitized and sympathetic works of
"friends of the Indian" such as La Farge, Ufer, and Waters. The images of the
Indian created by these Euramericans and Anglos have, until recently, been
those that have influenced the public perception of Indians, both among
Indians and non-Indians. With few exceptions, the identity of the Indian
has been written into the public consciousness by non-Indians, a situation
fostered by the imperatives of colonialism both to define and isolate the
alien Other and then to appropriate the identity of the colonized. Generally,
Indians have not been permitted to speak for themselves or, if they have,
their voices have been largely overlooked. As Edward Said notes,

> only recently have Westerners become aware that what they have
> to say about the history and the cultures of "subordinate" peoples
> is challengeable by the people themselves, people who a few years
> back were simply incorporated, culture, land, history, and all,
> into the great Western empires, and their disciplinary discourses.[1]

However, conspicuous by their discursive absence, Indians themselves have suffered an immense identity crisis that, besides being disabling and disenfranchising, contributes to their deracination and ultimately their cultural and/or physical genocide. To paraphrase Fanon, "at its extreme, the myth of the [Indian], the idea of the [Indian], can become the decisive factor in an authentic alienation."[2] With this in mind, it seems appropriate to turn our attention to emerging Indian voices attempting to articulate their own identities, both personal and cultural. Certainly, in the words of art critic and historian Lucy Lippard, "It is easier to think of all Americans moving toward whiteness and the ultimate shelter of the Judeo-Christian umbrella than to acknowledge the true diversity of this society."[3] But to do so is to accept only one side of the story behind the identity of the Indian, one couched in fantasies of the "master race."

When we realize that most "modern" white- and Indian-created art and literature addressing Indian themes is still cast in the same mold as that conceived by traditional western artists such as Frederick Remington, Charles Russell, Thomas Moran, and the Taos artists, or traditional storytellers such as Zane Gray, Longfellow, and Alan LeMay, the necessity of looking at modern Indian-created art and literature becomes even more pressing.

Much of both modern painting and sculpture on Indian themes seem frozen in the aesthetic traditions of the 1880s and 1930s. As Rennard Strickland writes in his essay of an imagined dialogue between modern Indian artists, gallery owners, and scholastic types, "More damned Indians have frozen to death in painted trails of tears than the white man ever killed."[4] An aura of nostalgia pervades modern western art, a nostalgia that is eminently commodified and self-conscious. The 1985 edition of *Contemporary Western Artists*, for instance, attests to this pernicious reality with particular charm. Designed to be a collector's handbook, this compilation of more than one hundred contemporary artists—mostly Euramericans, but including some Hispanics and Indians—contains a myriad of works whose influences in style, theme, and significance are easily traceable to much earlier times: the romanticized past of the Old West. The artists attest readily and unabashedly to these influences, as a few examples will divulge.

William Acheff, a trompe l'oeil painter of Indian artifacts, confesses that "I moved to Taos out of curiosity of the Southwestern art movement."[5] Mike Desatnick, who paints southwestern Indians in an impressionist style, finds "their beauty, character, and simplicity of life which harmonizes with nature to be very special in these sophisticated times."[6] Arlene Hooker Fay began by decorating her home "in 'early Indian' and decided to do a few Indian portraits to hang at home."[7] Burr Fairlamb, represented by an acrylic painting of an Indian winter encampment, explains: "I am addicted to giving my subjects nostalgic treatment, regardless of what they are. Certain tribes of American Indians had qualities that I find attractive in their everyday lives at the turn of the century, *rather than today*."[8] Image upon image of Indians posed in traditional dress, buffalo roaming the depopulated prairie, Puebloan villages in a variety of stylistic interpretations, Indian artifacts arranged in still lifes and more abstract motifs, buffalo hunts, picturesque ceremonial dances and tipi villages, and expansive desert vistas capturing the "magical New Mexico light" accumulate until one is almost overcome with a repulsive sense of commercial affluence and manipulation posing as historical authenticity. And make no mistake about it, these artists sell like hot fry bread at a cold powwow. As the compilers of this catalogue acknowledge, "This book establishes the cast of characters for investment in contemporary Western art by providing a list of artists who can be assumed to be *investment grade*."[9]

"When the real is no longer what it used to be," writes Baudrillard, "nostalgia assumes its full meaning":

> There is a proliferation of myths of origin and signs of reality; of second-hand truth, objectivity and authenticity. There is . . . a resurrection of the figurative where the object and substance have disappeared. And there is a panic-stricken production of the real and the referential, above and parallel to the panic of material production: this is how simulation appears in the phase that concerns us—a strategy of the real, the neo-real and the hyperreal whose universal double is a strategy of deterrence.[10]

What is being deterred, it seems, in these persistent reproductions of a nostalgic, market-driven aesthetic of the Indian is the archetypal power of Indians *in the present*. Ultimately, our search for a "real" Indian identity must be deferred to the articulations of real Indians who, bearing witness to their own psychic experience, give rise to their own archetypes as extracted from the pervasive trivialization and stereotyping of them over time. Even within Indian artistic and literary discourses, however, identity and identification are as allusive, elusive, and controversial as they are in white discourse, and any definitive characterization of Indianness must remain as impossible as that of "humanness" in general. More importantly, we must look to particular Indian artists and writers who express some degree of individual integrity that transcends the repetitive, the banal, and the mere reproduction of commodious Indian iconographies.

A BRIEF HISTORY OF THE INDIAN ARTIST

From the moment that the Indian subjects of the Taos Society artists "suddenly saw themselves as valuable parts of a profitable enterprise," and white entrepreneurs discovered the increasing marketability of "authentic" Indian products, a new partnership between them began to emerge. Indians themselves, who thus far had been relegated to reproducing artifacts for the Harvey House tourist trade in their traditional forms as pottery, weaving, basketry, and jewelry (among others in the Southwest), began to be encouraged into more European artistic media. The BIA administration of John Collier, instrumental in the Indian New Deal, also formed the Indian Arts and Crafts Board in 1935, designed to "enlarge the market for Indian arts and crafts, improve methods of production, and adopt a government trademark to protect goods made by Indians from imitation."[11]

Dorothy Dunn had already founded the Studio at the Santa Fe Indian School in 1932, where Indians were encouraged to paint scenes from their own tradition in the "flat-art" style that had developed among several artists of the San Ildefonso and Kiowa Reservations, and easel painting, along with the use of other nontraditional materials such as colored pencil, ledger book paper, watercolors, and illustration board among the Plains Indians (since the 1870s), began to emerge into the market as Indian "fine art," as opposed to "craft." For the stamp of authenticity implied by the Arts and Crafts Board to apply, however, certain images and styles "dictated by non-Indians, who dominate the art market, the field of criticism, and the administration of galleries and museums," had to be upheld.[12] The government imprimatur, while attempting to ensure that Indians got credit for their own work, also limited the context and content of that work to specific criteria that, like those of the "modern" western artists mentioned above, amounted to the continued reproduction of stereotypical Noble and Ignoble Savage themes for the collective non-Indian market, with the notable exception of Dunn's Studio. "In the Southwest (as evidenced in the pages of *Southwest Art* magazine [which also sponsored the publication by Samuels])," argues Gerhard Hoffman, "the lore of the Indian, the glamour of the cowboy, and the grandeur of the land are the paraphernalia of a regional art that has little to do with genuine Indian art."[13]

As a result of these restrictions, several Indian artists, wishing instead to find their own expressive identities apart from the influential but short-lived Dunn-style painting of the Santa Fe School, sought exposure to the wider field of international art forms. "One of the key issues of the controversy in Indian art today," observes Jamake Highwater, "is the undeniable fact that Indian artists are becoming progressively individualistic, rather than tribal, in their thinking and in their creative achievements."[14] Such individualism among Indian artists, just as that portrayed in the literature of La Farge and Waters, would inevitably lead to a new dynamism in Indian-created art that seeks to deconstruct stereotypes and reassert the archetypes inherent in the Indian experience: the "expressive imperative" enunciated by Highwater.

In part, this deconstruction has been accomplished by Indian artists who began to use nontraditional forms to portray Indian themes in new and idiosyncratic ways. Abandoning the conventions taught him by Dunn, Oscar Howe (Dakota Sioux) "returned from . . . duty in Europe during World War II with [the] radically new art ideal" of cubism, which he proceeded to apply to Indian subjects in a way that conjoined the new ideal with the long-standing tradition of Plains hide paintings and the ledger book drawings of Indian prisoners at Fort Marion, Florida, during the 1870s. As Howe explained to Highwater, "European modernism is intrinsic to the ancient Dakota Indian art style: 'The drawing-painting of the semi-abstract art is a two-dimensional rendering of object-idea.'"[15] Similarly, Howe's pupil Fritz Scholder (Luiseño), and Scholder's student T. C. Cannon (Kiowa-Caddo), adopted an expressionistic, pop art style to convey Indian-ness in new and ironic ways. Scholder's *Laughing Indian* (1973), for example, makes fun of the stereotypical idea of primitive stoicism through his highly deromanticized, grotesque Indian figure. Working against the grain of the romanticized, ethnologically frozen Indians of Karl Bodmer, who painted them in the 1830s, Scholder boldly caricatures Bodmer's Indians, creating humorous comment on the Noble Savage image.

Cannon, who was one of the first students at the BIA-established Institute of American Indian Arts in Santa Fe, founded in 1962, employed a similar tactic to that of his mentor, Scholder, synthesizing iconographies, styles, and ideologies from traditional Indian, Euramerican, and individual sources into impressively painted canvases, many of which are now, like Scholder's, extremely influential and widely collected. Cannon, who died in 1978 at the age of thirty-one, was himself an eclectic mix of "new wave Indian," Vietnam War veteran, rock lyricist, poet, and perennial innovator. His *Self Portrait in Studio* (1975), for instance, shows the artist dressed to the hilt in cowboy finery, clutching a "quiver" of paintbrushes (instead of arrows), against a backdrop of stylized southwestern scenery. On the wall behind him are a painting by Matisse and a poster of an African mask, icons of impressionism and cubism, respectively.[16]

Patrick Desjarlait (Ojibwa/Chippewa) was highly influenced by Mexican muralist Diego Rivera in his depictions of Indians as heroic workers. Woodrow Crumbo's (Creek/Potawatomi) *Land of Enchantment* (see p. 58) incorporates the illustrative style of East Coast journalists to comment wryly on the Southwest tourist trade, while most of his other highly innovative work is full of visionary grace and vibrant coloration reminiscent of Oriental art. Others were influenced by art nouveau and Matisse's decorative style (Cannon, Kevin Red Star), abstraction (Millard Dawa Lomakema, Jaune Quick-to-See Smith, Robert Davidson), and abstract expressionism (George Longfish, Dan Namingha).[17] By using European and American avant-garde techniques and styles in new ways, these Indian artists, whose subjects and motifs are still (usually) identifiably Indian, succeed in deflating the stereotypical romantic conventions of the early Indian and Taos Society studio painters. Traditional iconography gives way to new genres while still informing us of its Indian origins.

Conversely, other Indian artists have appropriated traditional forms such as pottery, weaving, hide paintings, jewelry, and pictography only to inject them with new revelations of context and meaning. Randy Lee White (Sioux) has recast traditional Ghost Dance shirts in handmade paper, illustrating them with typical flat-figured representations of quasi-historical events reflecting the "winter count" hide drawings of early Plains Indian culture. His *Custer's Last Stand Revisited* (1980) portrays in winter count style a modern event—the selling of junk cars to the Rosebud Sioux. While Robert Davidson, mentioned above as an abstractionist, has further abstracted the traditional "formline" styles of his native Haida culture, he also uses the traditional media of woodcarving, jewelry, totem poles, and masks to produce an eclectic blend of old forms with modernist feeling.[18] In a different vein, Jesse Cooday (Tlingit) overlays serigraphic images from traditional masks over photographs of living faces, often his own. Effie Garcia (Santa Clara) "has adapted the 1930s Santa Clara preference for deeply carved ceramic designs by introducing art deco–influenced geometries in place of the earlier curvilinear and animal motifs."[19] The medium, however, is easily identifiable as traditional, black-slipped Santa Clara pottery. Many other examples exist of both of these overlapping trends in modern Indian art, three of which I will discuss in depth below.

In short, the history of modern Indian art is one of exceeding complexity and diversity. Its concerns are both personal and cultural, historical and transhistorical, and as such modern Indian artists seek to reinvent themselves in a syncretic and volatile world where neither the medium nor the message is predictable. "The study of [Indian] arts is, par excellence, the study of changing arts," writes Hoffman, "of emerging ethnicities, modifying identities, and commercial and colonial stimuli and repressive actions."[20] By virtue of their very Otherness, Indian artists, having been both inoculated with some whiteness and given a new freedom with which to discover an antidote to that inoculation, live on the decisive edge of their alienation, knowing that, as stereotypes, they are forever condemned to a receding past. This alienation, like that of some modernist European painters and sculptors, allies Indian artists to some extent with the same existential angst that placed the European artists "at the center of the growing tensions between subject and object, individual and society, and between rational consciousness and the elemental impulses of the unconscious [from whence emerge the archetypes]." Thus we should not be surprised, advises Hoffman, to find Indian artists appropriating modernist styles and nontraditional media, for their "alienation . . . from the world, from society, and from reason results in a new spiritual quest."[21] While their own artistic traditions have been wantonly appropriated by non-Indians for commercial and artistic use, and their cultural symbolic heritage squandered through overcommercialization into triviality and cliché, modern Indian artists are forced, even with some renewed sense of freedom, to seek their identities in the idiosyncratic image banks of the collective unconscious and the transcultural consciousness of modernity and postmodernism.

In Highwater's essay "Controversy in Native American Art," one senses, as in Waters, an explicit undertone of the philosophical concepts of Jung, a resonance that helps Highwater to achieve a sense of universality and a helpful philosophical kinship with the present discussion. The concepts of Jung regarding the similarities and differences between what he calls the "personal unconscious" and the "collective unconscious," and the significance of their symbolic contents, play well in the controversy over what constitutes "Indian art" and what constitutes "art" in the broader world market. Jung's categories serve to highlight the tension between what might be meaningful as art only to traditional Indians and "Indian-loving" whites (that is, conservative sentimentalists and patrons), and what might be considered as more universal art that happens to be created by Indians. The latter might be said to correspond more closely to the "collective unconscious," while the former might align more with the "personal unconscious," at least with regard to how we are to assess their significance as art. Since Highwater echoes Jung's concern with "the process of individuation" that he perceives as being at the crux of the controversy, we might do well to briefly reconsider how Jung has perceived this process, especially as it pertains to symbolic content and the emergence of that content into the individual psyche of the artist.[22]

"Can the Indian image evolve from stereotype to archetype?" is the central concern not only of Highwater but also of Gerhard Hoffman, and the word *archetype* again returns us to a Jungian perspective.[23] Perhaps it would be more precise to ask, "Can the individual Indian artist retrieve the original archetypes from the mass of stereotypes that have taken over his or her consciousness, and project those archetypes in an individuated way upon the modern artistic consciousness at large?" Like artistic individuation in the sense Highwater seems to suggest, Jungian individuation is also "an experience in images and of images," with the most universally symbolic of those images being the archetypes, which pertain not to any particular race or ethnicity, as do racial stereotypes, but to a common human experience of the collective unconscious. We might say, then, that the conservative, traditional approach to Indian art is principally concerned with maintaining the homogeneous identity of the personal unconscious of the tribe, its unique symbols and images, while the emerging individuated Indian artist is more concerned with his or her relationship with the larger heterogeneous community of symbolic emotions that derive from the collective unconscious and are then filtered through that individual's consciousness. In addition, it should be noted that the recognition of one level does not preclude a recognition of the other, and that indeed both symbolic reservoirs can and do act together in creating individuated art.

As Lippard observes, however,

> [m]odernist Indian artists are often caught between cultures, attacked by their own traditionalists for not being Indian enough and attacked by the white mainstream for being "derivative," as though white artists hadn't helped themselves to things Indian [and African and Oriental as well] for centuries and as though Indians did not live (for better or worse) in the dominant culture along with the rest of us.[24]

The longer traditional Indian artists insist on the sanctity of their symbolic repertoire, and white patrons insist on the continued repetition of that repertoire as the only constituted "Indian art," the more that repertoire assumes a stereotypical and superficial significance, for it is being held in stasis as a determinant meaning and cannot reflect the evolution of the Indian psyche into postcontact reality. Jung says, speaking of still-potent cultural archetypes,

> Tribal lore is always sacred and dangerous. All esoteric teachings seek to apprehend the unseen happenings in the psyche, and all claim supreme authority for themselves. What is true of primitive lore is true in even higher degree of the ruling world religions.

In addition, archetypal symbols tend to lose their original power by repeated conscious use over time: "the more comprehensive the image that has evolved and been handed down by tradition, the further removed it is from individual experience. We can just feel our way into it and sense something of it, but the original experience has been lost."[25] How, then, can Indian artists restore primal power to their symbolic heritage?

Because we are speaking of significance and power in artistic imagery, we might imagine that, like the supernatural influences of the kachinas in Hopi culture, all archetypal images wax and wane in significance, depending on the historical consciousness in which they constellate. As Waters has said of the kachinas, "they appear and disappear with the ebb and flow of time, like life itself, and they are as legion as its infinite forms."[26] Kachinas who no longer carry mythopoetic meaning to the present culture are extracted from the ceremonial dance, or modified to accommodate new meanings, as are some of the hackneyed and defused traditional symbols from modern Indian art. Thus, when we analyze contemporary, nontraditional Indian artists, we must seek out the context as much as the form of the imagery being used, and decide how that imagery, whether traditional, modernist, idiosyncratically individuated, or all in combination, forms a new message in their art; and it may well form newly enunciated archetypes as well.

Three Indian artists—Jaune Quick-to-See Smith, Hachivi Edgar Heap of Birds, and Diego Romero—have formulated powerful new messages through the combined use of new and old forms, images, and signifiers. Together, their work seems to address a new concept of Indianness whose central, even archetypal, message is one of anger. But what makes their anger stimulating artistically is the way in which each, though their styles are vastly different, manipulates images and forms them into new constellations of meaning. If emotional content be the stuff of spirituality, as Jung has suggested, and the archetypes be symbols of emotion at the deepest level, and, further, if anger be such a primal emotion, then I think we can see in their work the emergence into consciousness, the articulation, of a central archetype of the modern, and historical, Indian: Anger with a capital *A*. If indeed this archetype is, as we know, not exclusively Indian, then its impact may be seen as a universal expression of the unconscious spirit of marginalized people everywhere, and thus as an example of the finest intentions of art, that is, those that render motifs of the unconscious into consciousness via the process of individuation. Anger, of course, is but one of a myriad of emotions that modern Indian artists portray, but it may be a central one not only to the inspiration and contextualization of their art, but also to its effectiveness as a discernible message. Anger against their bad postcontact history is an almost ubiquitous topic or theme in both Indian art and literature since the 1930s, and the various artists and writers discussed below amply illustrate that fact.

Agents of Oppression, one of three 1993 works in pottery by Diego Romero (Cochiti), serves as a fine example of the idiosyncratic and eclectic use of form and imagery that informs some modern Indian art. It also succinctly evokes the archetype of anger through significations that are startling and liable to anger the unwary viewer as well by their unexpected message. One

Cochiti ceramic artist Diego Romero's startling pieces *Agents of Oppression* (1993) and *The Drinker* (1993) make unabashed political statements about modern Indian life as influenced by white/Spanish civilization. (Courtesy of the artist, from the collection of the Denver Art Museum, Denver, Colorado.)

approaches Romero's pieces, on display in the traditional museum ambiance of pedestal and Plexiglas case, expecting yet another example of Mogollon/Cochise pottery presented as artifact. One of three shallow bowls is slightly tilted toward the viewer, its outside finished in a traditional red slip. Even as one approaches closer, one sees a traditional Acoma or Zia geometrical design, glazed in black, running around the inside lip of the pot; so far, nothing out of the ordinary. But once the eyes are drawn inevitably into the hollow of the vessel, there dwell images that shatter all complacent expectations. Three black-glazed figures comprise the composition: a Franciscan priest, a Spanish conquistador, and an abject Indian kneeling between them holding a cross. They stand/kneel on black ground, whose aggregate is interspersed with a skull and various pot shards, suggesting the archaic past, or perhaps the more recent murderous past; above them hangs a black cloud figure with rain streaks, infusing the stormy present. Like the encircling design, the scene is rendered in a simple, stylized line, but the symbolic "contents" of the bowl shatter its form by an act of sheer incongruity, making the viewer shudder with his or her own conventional expectations that "Indian art" is nonpolitical, aboriginally innocent, and emotionally harmless. One sees not the simple beauty of stylized nature, a romantic simplicity we expect from aboriginal art, but rather evidence of a human atrocity committed in the name of God upon both the art and the heritage of Amerindian people. The spiritual simplicity of the form is broken by an archetypal image of oppression, and the consciousness of the viewer is propelled into new realizations about the fate of Mogollon potters, of Mogollon cosmology, and of Indian history as affected by the moment of contact. From that fracture between stereotypical form and archetypal image rises a powerful message of anger.

Two other pieces by Romero accomplish similar feats of grotesque juxtaposition. *Coyote and the Disciples of Vine Deloria Jr.* and *The Drinker* both play on other aspects of enculturation and oppression. The Coyote bowl contains the image of two Indians and a coyote figure riding in a pickup truck; the coyote is drinking from a bottle, while one Indian drives and the other sits in the bed of the truck toting a machine gun. While more serendipitous than the previous message, with the drinking trickster/coyote, the machine gun, and the pickup truck denoting a kind of directionless rage, this image also rings with a demystified, historical reality that confounds its "beautiful" form. In *The Drinker*, an Indian with bottle to mouth sits on the same charred ground as in the other pieces, dying on the mound of his primal history at the hands of the heady liquor of the oppressor. It sends a message of spiritual degradation, its traditionally spiritual form having been laid in dark contrast to the degrading "spirits" of reservation liquor runners.

All three pieces resonate to the conflagration of cultural and historical disparity, the breaking of a lineage of significance by new signifiers of oppression and disjuncture. Incidentally, perhaps, in all three pieces the initial, traditional designs around the lips of the pots, usually designed to run unbroken (like a "spirit line") in a continuum, are not conjoined where their pattern should meet, as if the oppressor had entered the context of the bowls through an error in "design." Romero, using traditional media combined with a modern message, thus opens up a new and powerful dialectic between the two that sends an archetypal message of angry resistance.

In the "word drawings" of Edgar Heap of Birds (Cheyenne-Arapaho), the preceding relationship between form and image is practically reversed; that is, the archetypal message of anger emerges when traditional, linguistic images from the personal unconscious of the artist take the modern form of word drawings, a form traceable in European art to dadaism and surrealism. Heap of Birds's piece *He No Wah Maun Stun He Dun (What Makes a Man? Self)* (1988) consists of fifteen panels of pastel on rag paper, each containing two to four words in English rendered in frenetically drawn letters of different colors. The whole is constituted by hanging the panels next to each other, three horizontally and five vertically. The effect of this work seems akin to that of the "cut-up" technique used in collagist writing by William S. Burroughs and Brion Gysin. Before them, similar techniques were practiced by the early surrealist Tristan Tzara in the 1920s. In their practice of the technique (from the 1960s on):

> Take any poet or writer you fancy, or your own journalistic scribblings. The words have lost meaning and life through years of repetition. Fill a page with excerpts. Now cut the page into four or eight equal sections and rearrange the pieces at random. You have a new poem, as many poems as you like.[27]

"Reading" Heap of Birds's piece requires a similar method: one can read the words on each panel consecutively, or read across from left to right just the top words on each panel, or read from groups of words together into other groups of words vertically, horizontally, diagonally, or at random, and differ-

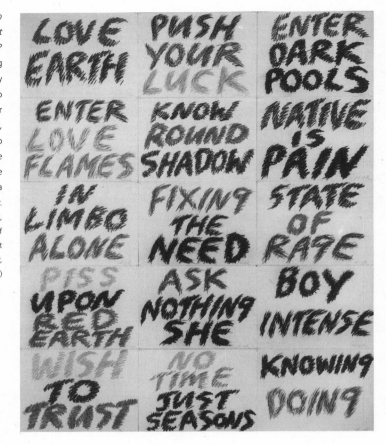

ent poems and images emerge from each reading method (or nonmethod). Considering each panel as a "phrase" with its own self-contained meaning, for instance, we find that there are contextual similarities between, say, panel 1 ("LOVE/EARTH") and panels 10 ("PISS/UPON/RED/EARTH") and 14 ("NO/TIME/JUST/SEASONS"), in that they all relate to "nature" and the way Indianness, perhaps, relates to nature. In contrast, we find that panels 3 ("ENTER/DARK/POOLS"), 4 ("ENTER/LOVE/FLAMES"), 5 ("KNOW/ROUND/SHADOW"), and 13 ("WISH/TO/TRUST") all hint at something metaphysical or mystical about Indian life. Obviously, there are endless "readings" of this piece, some making more "sense" than others, and the mind of the viewer is thus engaged in making meaning and identity from the linguistic artifacts that appear before him or her.

The fact that no particular reading yields a determinant meaning for the piece implies something about Indian identity, and perhaps about human identity in general; successive readings either reinforce or deconstruct each other, producing a sense of vertiginous uncertainty about identity, but never any particular identity. These "unembellished texts," writes Lippard about this same piece, "leave gaps that refer to and bounce off social gaps and outrages."[28] The resulting message, then, is rather like a whirling dervish of significations, at whose vortex lies an emotion derived from such instability, anger: "STATE/OF/RAGE," "BOY/INTENSE," "NATIVE/IS/PAIN." Because the singular messages evoke the broken image of Indian identity, of Indian ego, and are rendered in a postmodern form that further enunciates that brokenness, the viewer witnesses a Jungian intrusion of the unconscious into the seemingly symmetrical form of the whole, inducing what Hoffman has characterized as "a loss of even that fragile subjectivity [in the form of identity] as an integrating principle and its substitution by decentralized fields of experience, or 'situations.' "[29] As such, the piece exhibits a universalized disparity and vertigo that tie it to the postmodern. By virtue of Heap of Birds's manipulation of traditional Indian sentiments into a decontextualized melange of meanings, the work indeed begs the question: "What Makes a Man?" Here, language (even the metalanguage of myth) cannot offer any determinant meaning to Indianness.

The simple pictorial forms of the famed ledger book art of the Fort Marion artists, with their emphases on costume and on historical reenactment, come into modern use in the work of Jaune Quick-to-See Smith (Cree-Flathead-Shoshone). Ledger books were given to Plains Indian prisoners in Florida in the 1870s, on which several of them recaptured the "splendid picture-writing tradition of the Plains Indians."[30] However, as in Romero, this traditional form supplies the stereotype against which the archetype of anger resonates into consciousness. At first, her work *Paper Dolls for a Post-Colombian World with Ensembles Created by the U.S. Government* (1991) seems playfully benign and harmlessly decorative, like the Fort Marion pieces by Buffalo Meat, Howling Wolf, and others. At the top of the piece, rendered in crayon on paper, are the principal characters portrayed as cutout paper dolls: Father Le De Ville (as in "the devil"), the Jesuit priest, and the Indian family of Ken, Barbie, and Bruce Plenty Horses.

Below these figures are various costumes and accessories that one can, in imagination, also cut out and impose over the Indian characters. But the playfulness of the form and its historical antecedents soon yield to disturbing images provided by the accompanying text written alongside each "ensemble" and "accessory," and a sense of semiological seriousness overrides the childlike concept.

What does Smith's use of the paper doll concept actually suggest about Indian identity? For one thing, it suggests that Indians have been the historical "toys" of the U.S. government. It further insinuates that Indians are as capable of being manipulated as are the Ken and Barbie dolls of popular culture, and that their postcontact history is one of political manipulation. Semiologically, these suggestions coalesce to signify that the American Indian identity has been one "cut out" by the dominating culture, who, by a mere inflexion in ideology, and abetted by nefarious political action, have "cut down" the Indian into subjugation and potential extinction.

This message is further communicated by the accompanying text, which explains how each successive "costume change" on the unadorned Indians led to a further deterioration of their self-image and their image in the eyes of white Christian culture. By one change, Ken Plenty Horses is transformed into a drinker of gunpowder-laden whiskey, who signs away his tribal land ("Special outfit for trading land with the U.S. Government for whiskey with gunpowder in it"); by another, son Bruce is deprived of his religious heritage at the BIA Indian school, then trained to be a common laborer in the white economy; and mother Barbie is transformed into a household servant, since she can no longer grow crops on her own land after relocation ("Maid's uniform for cleaning houses of white people after good education at Jesuit school or gov't. school"). Smallpox-ridden blankets sent to the reservations provide ensembles of red dots for the whole family, and a ration box accessory contains poisoned or poisoning "commodity food," still a staple for many living on reservations. Meanwhile, Father Le De Ville perches at the top of the composition, his vestments intact, with dollar signs fluttering about him, while below him the Indians descend into degradation.

The power of Quick-to-See Smith's work seems to lie in its conflation of traditional forms and stereotypical notions of the facile Indian with an acute, unflattering, and blackly humorous evocation of the author of such forms and notions, the white Christian hegemony. She suggests, quite rightly, that many non-Indian notions of Indianness are devoid of any human or historical connotations, and that they spring from a capital-driven economy augmented by Christian dogma. That Amerindians have been dehumanized to the point of being mere toys upon which one can project necessarily stereotypical illusions and degraded images of Otherness is a process rightly confronted by Smith. Her forms play on our own naiveté about "Indian art" and Indianness, while the tragic images she evokes from them confront us with the residual anger of the oppressed.

As modern Apache artist Bob Haozous has maintained, "legitimate art is generated from the individual Native American experience, not from slavish adherence to ethnically prescribed styles or subjects."[31] While all three of these artists have "quoted" something stereotypically "Indian" in their work (Romero, traditional pottery form; Heap of Birds, traditional philosophical sentiment; and Smith, traditional Plains pictorial style), they have also repudiated and/or transformed these references through an invocation of their own individuated experience into archetypal symbols of anger, an archetype that transcends ethnic limitations. Surely both Indian and non-Indian witnesses to their art can share the emotions being invoked, and acknowledge that a Foucaultian "crack" has opened between the stereotyped Indian and the individuated Indian artist into whose conventionally ordered consciousness has irrupted the archetype of anger. That this anger must be dealt with in consciousness, through art, is the imperative of individuation as Waters, Highwater, Hoffman, and Jung perceive it: "The archetype is essentially an unconscious content that is altered by becoming conscious and by being perceived, and it takes its colour from the individual consciousness in which it happens to appear."[32] Thus, these Indian artists, whose heritage is steeped in shamanism and symbolism, find again in the modern world their ancient struggle with the unconscious, and seek to enlighten the human tribe in their modern capacity as artists.

TRANSFORMING THE ORAL TRADITION

> My parentage, according to the custom of the country, was none of the least—
> being the descendent of a chief, or the head officer of the nation. But this
> availed nothing with me; the land of my fathers was gone; and their characters
> were not known as human beings but as beasts of prey. We were represented as
> having no souls to save, or to lose, but as partridges upon the mountains. All
> these degrading titles were heaped upon us. Thus, you see, we had to bear all
> this tide of degradation, while prejudice stung every white man, from the oldest
> to the youngest, to the very center of the heart.
>   *William Apess,* The Experiences of Five Christian Indians of the Pequot
>   Tribe

Like their counterparts in the pictorial arts, modern Indian writers also have
been involved in the struggle to bring authenticity and individuality into a
context of Indianness that is both tradition-based and attuned to the processes and forms of the modern world. Before the English language was
thrust upon them as an enculturating array of confusing and unintelligible
new ideas and concerns, Indian tribes had had an immemorial history of
oral tradition which, more like the ancient drama of storytelling of Homer
and Ovid than like the Western literary canon, remained all the more vivid
because of its nonmaterial form—it was a tradition of performance and
dramaturgy that included vocal and gestural inflexion, spontaneous im-
provisation, the rhythm of drums and rattles, the coincidental meanings of
certain ceremonial times of the year, and the drama of human presence and
audience participation. On certain occasions, the drama was further height-
ened when stories and songs were performed as part of a ritual celebration or
sacred ceremony, such as the Navajo Night Chant or the Iroquois Ritual of
Condolence (among hundreds of others). Storytelling, song, and prayer
combined to form a vigorous cultural and spiritual literary tradition that was
not separated from daily life as a discrete "art," as was the Western canon,

but rather formed the living matrix of expression between and within tribal communities. As Vera Laski learned from her Tewa associate, Shaayet'aan,

> [t]he purpose of our ceremonies is not entertainment but attainment; namely the attainment of the *Good Life*. Our dramas, our songs, and our dances are not performed for fun as they might be in the white man's world; no, they are more than that: they are the very essence of our lives; they are sacred.[1]

Not committed to the written word until relatively recently, Indian "literary" tradition arose spontaneously with the development of language and remains elastic and extemporaneous up unto the present.

With the coming of the colonists, the processes of deracination and enculturation slowly eroded the embedded values of the oral tradition. As we have seen, both governmental agencies and missionary Christians largely perceived Indian ceremonialism as primitive, heathenish, and even satanic, and sought to suppress not only the major ceremonials where their poetry might be heard, but also the storytelling and other oral transmissions of medicine men, shamans, and tribal elders. The eradication of Indians' native tongues was the goal of some missionary and government boarding schools, where children were isolated from their families and sometimes beaten for speaking their own language. In short, many Indians were shamed or beaten into forsaking or camouflaging their tribal languages, the only languages they had for remembering and retaining their tribal identities. Oral traditions obviously need audiences and participants within the community, talkers and hearers, who conjoin in continuously reinventing the culture in which they live. Without such community, confirmed by language, Indians were forced into a position of articulating their individual Indianness via the white man's language, a complex and initially confounding process.

The first such instances of this phenomenon were "autobiographies" of Native subjects, essentially "bicultural composite compositions."

> [T]hese texts are the end-products of a rather complex process involving a three-part collaboration between a white editor-amanuensis who edits, polishes, revises, or otherwise fixes the "form" of the text in writing, a Native "subject" whose orally presented life story serves as the "content" of the autobiographical

narrative, and in almost all cases, a mixed-blood interpreter/ translator whose exact contribution to the autobiographical project remains one of the least understood aspects of Indian autobiography.[2]

Ostensibly, the first such autobiography was produced, at least in part, by Mohegan Reverend Samson Occom in 1768, but it was not published until 1827. Two years later, the famous *A Son of the Forest: The Experience of William Apess a Native of the Forest, Written by Himself,* by William Apess, a mixed-blood Pequot, appeared. Since then and up to the present day, various permutations of the editor-subject-translator triumvirate of Indian autobiography and "autohistory" have made up a large part of the canon of Native literature; much has been written about the value of at least some of this canon in terms of authenticity and authorship, with arguments going back and forth. Distinctions, however tenuous, have been made between "ethnographic" and "literary" autobiographies, and between preliterate (oral and pictorial) and literate forms that might constitute official autobiography. Both Hertha D. Wong and H. David Brumble III argue that such artifacts as Sioux "winter count" hide paintings, rock art, and "coup tales" be included in the genre, and that the reader needs to bear in mind that the "focus [of Indian self-conception] is on a communal self who participates within the tribe," rather than on a more Western self that is more individualized and independent.[3] Others, such as Gretchen Bataille and Kathleen Sands, seek to confine the genre to those "literary" autobiographies that meet Western criteria. However one approaches these varied works, it is possible to glean for oneself a sense of their inherent worth and interest regarding Indian identities both precontact and modern. In reading the early "as told to" autobiographies, however, we should be aware, as Brumble cautions, that "[s]uch autobiographies usually are, in an important sense, bicultural documents, texts in which the assumptions of Indian autobiographers and Anglo editors are at work."[4]

Necessarily, many of the first autobiographies were by Christianized Indians who had learned English and adopted white ways. Some, such as Catharine Brown, a Cherokee convert, had become so de-Indianized that their most pressing sentiments regarding their own cultures were those of horror and denial: "When I think and see the poor thoughtless Cherokees going on in sin, I cannot help blessing God, that he has led me in the right path to serve him."[5] Other accounts, such as those of Black Hawk (Sac-Fox, 1833), Wooden Leg (Cheyenne, 1931), and Yellow Wolf (Nez Perce, 1908, published 1940), were the stories of the resisters and their chiefs. Other significant and highly influential "as told to" autobiographies were those of Geronimo, Black Elk, Luther Standing Bear, and Edmund Nequatewa, a Hopi chief. Journalists, anthropologists, and others concerned with preserving some vestige of the ostensibly vanishing Indian culled hundreds of somewhat less reliable life stories from just about any Indian who would talk to them. Nonetheless, the net effect of such works was to form a wedge of recognition that helped open the public consciousness to the rich realities of Indian life and history and to change the way American Indian history was viewed and written about.

Following the self-authored works by Occum and Apess was *Life Among the Paiutes: Their Wrongs and Claims,* by Paiute Indian activist Sarah Winnemucca Hopkins, in 1883. Based on a series of chastising lectures that Hopkins delivered to sympathetic white audiences, the book mixes personal and tribal histories with letters and other documentation. With her book's political ramifications largely overlooked and, as it turned out, misguided in that they supported the General Allotment Act of 1887, Hopkins "lost faith in the power and desire of the government to protect Indian land," and she died in poverty in 1887.[6] In 1900, Francis LaFlesche published *The Middle Five: Indian Schoolboys of the Omaha Tribe,* a poignant narrative of the Omaha Indian boy's life at the Presbyterian Mission School in Bellevue, Nebraska. Of great interest in the following years are assimilationists Charles Eastman's *From the Deep Woods to Civilization: Chapters in the Autobiography of an Indian* (1916) and Gertrude Bonnin's *Impressions of an Indian Childhood* (1900), and the memoirs written by the Oxford-educated John Joseph Matthews, an Osage, which were published in 1945 as *Talking to the Moon: Wildlife Adventures on the Plains and Prairies of Osage Country.*

Foremost among later self-autobiographers are those of the so-called Native American Renaissance, beginning after 1968: N. Scott Momaday (*The Way to Rainy Mountain* [1969] and *The Names: A Memoir* [1976]), Linda Hogan ("The Two Lives" [1987]), Leslie Marmon Silko (*Storyteller* [1981]), and Gerald Vizenor (*Interior Landscapes: Autobiographical Myths and Metaphors* [1990] and "Crows Written on the Poplars: Autocritical Autobiographies" [1987]), along with numerous semi- or wholly autobiographical poems by such noted modern writers as Simon Ortiz, Carter Revard, Adrian C. Louis, Sherman Alexie, and Wendy Rose.[7]

Autobiography, oddly enough, became the literary vehicle through which many Indian fiction and poetry writers would eventually gain an audience. I say "oddly," because the notion of the importance of an individual life history, or even a consciousness, apart from the tribal community at large, was not an intrinsically Indian one. For any Indian to suspect that his or her own personal experiences would be of any autonomous value was foreign to most of them until it became clear (to some) that the individualism that was part and parcel of white civilization could form the basis for a literary career as well as a clarification of one's own identity, albeit in the language of the Other. This tension between the communal experience of the tribe and the unique experience of the individual has its parallel in that between traditionalism and individuation, as we have come to understand it in this discussion. Certainly these are tensions that all Westernized individuals undergo in the maturation process from a family orientation to one with the society at large, and finally with one's self as an semiautonomous entity within the social amalgam as a whole.

Those Indians who wish to understand and participate in their relationship with Western, Americanized civilization have further had to cross the threshold between cultural isolation within their own tribes and a wider intellectual involvement with the issues brought forth by that relationship. For some who became and are becoming "authors" in the Western sense of the word, this has meant education, scholarly practice, gaining credence within the circle of extant Indian writers and the Indian intellectual tradition, and finding a literary voice that is at once Indian and "authorial" as defined by Western concepts. The latter definition largely resides in the publishability of Indian writing as decided by the marketeers of the industry. Besides the autobiographical form, they have also ventured into the alien literate forms of novelistic and short-story fiction, poetry, playwriting, journalism, song lyrics, and screenplay writing. The most successful have adopted the forms, but not necessarily the traditional motifs, of the Western canon, and have often brought to these genres the distinctive storytelling traditions of their own culture.

Among some of the significant stylistic hallmarks of Native writing today are the use of repetition, the recasting of tribal narratives into modern-day story lines, a certain admixture of sacred and profane influences, and the enunciation of tacitly Indian worldviews and personal experiences. The result is often a highly idiosyncratic blend of English language and forms with Indian sentiments and insights, wherein Indian writers use the power of the written word to deconstruct thematically the power of the written word, especially as it has been applied to them historically as a tool of colonialism. For many, writing is now a tool of decolonization and the discourse of intellectual, cultural, and political sovereignty. For others, it is an opportunity to reinvoke the poetry of the oral tradition, and thus a whole cultural ethos, so that it can once again flourish in a new medium and even change the medium itself. For all, it is another chance at authorship, authority, and authenticity that, once taken, can redeem that which was lost to shame, disfigurement, and oppression, in order to re-form vital identities.

A BRIEF HISTORY OF THE INDIAN WRITER

The first of nine American Indians to write fiction in the style of the Western canon prior to 1968 was John Rollin Ridge (Cherokee), who was among those on the Trail of Tears during the Cherokee Removal from their eastern homeland to the Indian Territory of Oklahoma. The Cherokee had been among the most cooperationist and assimilationist Indians of the earlier century, with many taking an active role in American business and politics, but they were betrayed by Jacksonian treachery. Thinking that the only way to save their tribe from military extirpation was to take the advice of Washington bureaucrats, Ridge's grandfather, Major, then a powerful leader among the Cherokee, and father, John Sr., were instrumental in signing away their ancestral lands; both were later assassinated for doing so. Eschewing a particularly Indian identity, Ridge wrote of the trials and revenge of a mixed-blood Mexican in *The Life and Adventures of Joaquin Murietta, the Celebrated California Bandit,* which was published in 1854. The novel is a picaresque western adventure based on the resistance of California Natives to the incursion of whites brought on by the gold rush and, in the opinion of literary historian A. Lavonne Brown Ruoff, is linked in style and influence "both to Gothic romances and Byron's narrative poems in English literature and to the frontier romances and dime-novel Westerns of American literature."[8] The publication of *Queen of the Woods* by Simon Pokagon (Potawatomi), "the first novel about Indian life written by an Indian," followed in 1899.[9] Perhaps the first novel to be concerned with an Indian-specific identity crisis was *Cogewea: The Half-Blood*, by the Okanagon-Colville woman writer Mourning Dove, published in 1927. A migrant farmworker, Mourning Dove wrote passionately about the dissociative identity crisis of a mixed-blood woman who, like Jackson's Ramona, must struggle within her own blood to find herself. *Cogewea* is often seen by modern scholars as a groundbreaking progenitor to much of modern Indian fiction, concerned as it is with blood quantum as a discursive element of identity, with the dissolution of Indian stereotypes, and with the search for particularly Indian perspectives and personalities bound up in its characterizations. According to mixed-blood author and critic Louis Owens (Choctaw-Cherokee-Irish),

> With its introduction of Cogewea as "a breed!—the socially ostracized of two races," Mourning Dove's novel announced explicitly what was to become the dominant theme in novels by Indian authors: the dilemma of the mixed-blood, the liminal "breed" seemingly trapped between Indian and white worlds.[10]

Similarly, Paula Gunn Allen (Laguna Pueblo-Sioux) notes that "*Cogewea* draws from protest and ceremonial themes to clarify the struggle for identity that characterizes Native writing in the United States in the twentieth century."[11]

Another Cherokee writer, John Milton Oskison, published three novels in the 1920s and 1930s—but only one, *Brothers Three,* incorporates major Indian characters. Better known, and certainly more compelling, are the fictional works of the Osage scholar-writer John Joseph Mathews, who left the Oklahoma "blackjack" country reservation in 1917 to serve in the U.S. Signal Corps in World War I, thus beginning a life of achievement and scholarship in the Anglo world. Mathews went on to get a B.A. from Oxford in 1923, attended the School for International Affairs, and traveled extensively in Europe, the Middle East, and North Africa. But after it all, he became homesick for his Native culture: "Why don't I go back and take some interest in my people?" he wrote in his journal. "Why not go back to the Osages? They've got culture."[12] Upon returning, he took up residence in "a small sandstone house on his allotment land," eight miles from Pawhuska, Oklahoma, which he nicknamed "The Blackjacks" after "the running scrub oak that dominates the landscape of that part of the Osage."[13]

Reimmersing himself in his own culture, Mathews got lucky immediately, when an Indian agent's journal fell into his hands. Written in the transitional period during which the Osage were forced onto the reservation, the journal provided the raw material from which Mathews wrote *Wah'Kon-Tah: The Osage and the White Man's Road,* a historical novel published in 1932. The book launched his literary career when it was chosen as a Book-of-the-Month Club selection. His novel *Sundown* followed in 1934, but it has only recently begun to receive critical attention. Also about a mixed-blood character, named Challenge Windzer, *Sundown* is a devastating political novel that chronicles one progressive Indian activist's disillusionment with U.S. politics and Indian-American relationships. Challenge's father, John, determined to make his son conversant in the hopeful (at the time) realities of assimilation into the larger hegemony, sends him to university and encourages him to engage in white society. This engagement, both at school and in the military, is tragically one-sided, however, and "Chal" ends up hating himself and his race and descends into drunken dishevelment. The novel ends ambiguously, with Chal somewhat restored to his Osage self, but still contemplating going to law school. "*Sundown* is not," however, as Robert Allen Warrior (Osage) points out, "a story of the conflict between white and Indian values [as some critics have made it out to be], but a nuanced description of what Mathews saw as the weaknesses of two internal political and social strategies in the midst of an oppressive situation."[14] Such social realism has come to set modern Native writing apart from the romanticized versions of Indian life that dominated earlier works by both Indians and non-Indians, and, as Owens says,

> Mathews leaves open the possibility of "another destiny, another plot" for the American Indian, refusing any romantic closure that would deny the immense difficulties confronting the displaced Native American, but simultaneously rejecting the cliché of the Vanishing American as epic, tragic hero.[15]

Owens is particularly insightful in noting that the major semiological and thematic thrust of modern Indian writing lies in the writer's appropriation of an alien language to recast the themes and plots heretofore assigned Indian characters by Anglo writers and "emphatically [make of] the Indian the hero of other destinies, other plots."[16]

Another major voice emerging around the same time as Mathews was D'Arcy McNickle (Flathead-Salish). Generally considered a more polished fiction writer than Mathews, McNickle was also to become a major guiding force in the Indian Reorganization programs of John Collier, under the FDR administration. His biography of Oliver La Farge, *Indian Man,* is exemplary of the congenial tone that characterized Indian-white intellectual relations during that time. His novels, however, are persuasively reflective of the difficulties that were also ubiquitous. *The Surrounded,* published in 1936, "remains one of the finest novels by a Native American writer."[17] While both Mathews and McNickle reveled in the influence of Hemingway, it is McNickle whose style most honors his precision and storytelling skill. Rife with the complicated influences of Catholic priests and white bureaucrats on Native culture, *The Surrounded* paints a claustrophobic portrait of passively confused and confounded Indians innocently being manipulated by these greater powers. The metalanguage of Christian myth successfully supersedes the traditional worldview of the Salish characters, beginning with the indoctrination of the mission school and continued under the guise of paternalism and civilization. The protagonist, Archilde Leon (perhaps a clever allusion to "our children," as the white missionaries thought of their wards), no matter what he might conceive of as proper acculturation, never finds his own way, even through assimilation. He is forever "imprisoned by America's image of the Indian" as an unempowered Other, incapable of making the transition to "civilized" society.[18] McNickle followed eighteen years later with a second novel, *Wind from an Enemy Sky,* that continues his interest in how Native and non-Native cultures can interact, if only they can learn to communicate with each other. Unfortunately for most of McNickle's Indian characters, the gnawing perplexity and emotional baggage that surround such communication usually result in tragedy, miscommunication, and death. McNickle's personal and professional involvement in the sociological and philosophical nuances of white-Indian affairs contributes much to the depth and authenticity of his writing, and his brilliant use of the language drives the points home to the non-Indian reader with powerful veracity.

When we speak of the so-called Native American Renaissance, we do so in reference to the publication in 1968 of Kiowa scholar and writer N. Scott Momaday's *House Made of Dawn,* which won the Pulitzer Prize for fiction in 1969. Perhaps one of the most beautifully written works of American fiction of this century, *House Made of Dawn* attracted worldwide attention to the social realities of Indians during and after the crude governmental policies of relocation and termination, as a result of which they were faced with tribal dissolution, disenfranchisement, dispersion into the urban diaspora, and exposure to the wholesale social evils of ruthless capitalism and world war. If one can imagine a sustained work of fiction written with the elocutionary power of Emily Dickinson, who was an inspiration and resource for Momaday, one can get an idea of the artistic accomplishment that *House Made of Dawn* achieves. Deeply evocative of Native culture and psychic ambiance, the novel traces the descent into personal hell of the Pueblo Indian Abel (or "Abelito," as his grandfather calls him), an orphaned boy subjected to the death of his brother, the horrors of World War II, and then to those of relocation into a dark urban environment. In essence the work is, like La Farge's *Laughing Boy,* a sociological probing into the complex and usually deleterious effects of white culture on Indian individuals and societies, this time from a thoroughly Indian point of view. Significantly, Abel is somehow, via the persistent strength of his inner Indian self, able to redeem himself to his Indian nature by the end of the book, announcing for all to see the viability of the survival of Indianness in a world bent on its destruction. As Owens has said of Abel's salvation:

> To be integrated into the pueblo—the people, the place—is to be timeless, outside of time and part of the endless cycle of nature. It is also to be removed from the experience of ephemerality, fragmentation, and deracination that characterizes the modern predicament and, most significantly, to be defined according to eternal, immutable values arising from a profound integration with place.[19]

With the acceptance and praise that followed *House Made of Dawn,* it seemed that a newer and wider audience had suddenly materialized for the fiction and poetry of Indian authors who incorporated into their methods the ancient storytelling techniques and motifs of their traditional, oral way. Both Native and non-Native critics recognize it as a watershed of Native American writing, as authentic in its origins and style as it is in its social realism. The warrior of Indian society is successfully rendered as a modern, even postmodern, hero, who undergoes successive deprivations and tortures typical, not of Greco-European literary heroes, but of real Indians existing in a historical maelstrom of social and psychic disjuncture and dissociation. And it must be said that the saving grace of Abel lies in his deeply ingrained Indian nature, dependent on his identification with the mythic Bear and

Eagle clans of his heritage for his final ability to avoid, rather than attack, the "snakes" of his destruction. Steeped in Navajo and Tanoan cultural lore, Abel's psychic life is redeemed by them as he himself is redeemed to the ancient way, couched in a "house made of dawn."

Two other major Indian writers, James Welch (Blackfoot-Gros Ventre) and Leslie Marmon Silko (Laguna), followed through the door left open by Momaday into prominence in American literature. Welch's *Winter in the Blood* (1974) and *The Death of Jim Loney* (1979) and Silko's *Ceremony* (1977) continue the examination of Indian displacement and salvation in the modern world, with distinctive and instinctive touches of their own. Welsh's unnamed first-person narrator has been described as a modern-day Fisher King by both Owens and Kenneth Lincoln, author of *Native American Renaissance,* a pivotal critical study. "Getting through is the novel's staying power," comments Lincoln, "taking courage from a direct language of words-as-things-are."

> The novel's chapters seem chiseled like petroglyphs, isolated in starkly precise planes. Scenes string out on a wire of pain just short of breaking, and the reader sees by glimpses, moment by moment, as the narrative almost fails to cohere and go on. Because and in spite of its fragmentation, its despair and loss, the story [like that of Abel] involves the reader in the struggle to survive.[20]

Similarly, Silko's *Ceremony,* though both more darkly witchy and more redemptive than Welch's work, charts the modern sickness of the mixed-blood Indian soul and, by extension, the sensitized white soul in their search for a postmodern identity amongst the ruins of bad history run amok. The "ceremony" of the title is the divine psychic process of the redemption of Silko's protagonist, Tayo, another Indian returned home from the war to face his own despoliation and dissipation, acted out in delusional schizophrenia, alcoholism, and inchoate barbarity. In the works of Momaday, Welch, and Silko, Indian characters are besieged by the modern "sickness," an existential condition reminiscent of Sartre's or Camus's inculcation and distillation of twentieth-century evil as, for instance, "nausea" or "the plague." Provoked by hideous war experiences, dissociative social conditions, cultural disenfranchisement, and psychic breakdowns exacerbated by alcoholism and the desensitization of failed love and communication, these modern Indian characters assume a universality that places the discussion of modern Indian life in the context of the massive dystopia of worldwide postcolonial fragmentation and breakdown. In response, their authors offer up some distinctively Indian engineering toward these characters', and thus all of our, survival.

Silko, in *Ceremony*, sees the sickness thusly:

> They all had explanations; the police, the doctors at the psychiatric ward, even Auntie and old Grandma; they blamed liquor and they blamed the war.
>
> "Reports note that since the Second World War a pattern of drinking and violence, not previously seen before, is emerging among Indian veterans." But Tayo shook his head when the doctor finished reading the report. "No?" the doctor said in a loud voice.
>
> "It's more than that. I can feel it. It's been going on for a long time."
>
> "What do you think it is?"
>
> "I don't know what it is, but I can feel it all around me."[21]

Silko intimates, through her interspersed cosmogenic ministries based on Laguna legend, that the real sickness is the result of one losing one's way, forgetting the essential stories of Indian identity when it was part and parcel of the ongoing oral tradition of storytelling and, with that, forgetting how to live. *Ceremony* is her way of recovering that tradition of spontaneously creating life and life stories as one went along, instead of letting them stagnate and become evil, via the "witchery" of the destroyers:

> The witchery would be at work all night so that the people would see only the losses—the land and the lives lost—since the whites came; the witchery would work so that the people would be fooled into blaming only the whites and not the witchery. It would work to make the people forget the stories of the creation and continuation of the five worlds; the old priests would be afraid too, and cling to ritual without making any new ceremonies as they always had before, the way they still make new Buffalo Dance songs each year.[22]

The witchery, like all human evil, is the obverse of the "ceremony" by which living cultures and identities are formed, and by which Indian characters in fiction and poetry transcend the witchery of projection, stereotyping, and the conjured-up white histories that they now defy.

Since 1968, more than one hundred Native writers have appeared in print in some form or another—as poets, fiction writers, and scholars—and their influence on the American psyche has grown considerable and even essential to the ongoing discourse that is American society at the end of the twentieth century. These "now day Indi'ns," as Lincoln has called them, also include Grey Cohoe (Navajo), Paula Gunn Allen (Laguna-Sioux), E. K. Caldwell (Cherokee-Creek-Shawnee-Celtic and German), Elizabeth A. Woody (Navajo-Warm Springs-Wasco-Yakima), Louise Erdrich (Chippewa-German-French), Gerald Vizenor (Chippewa-Ojibway), Louis Owens (Choctaw-Cherokee-Irish), Jim Northrup (Anishinaabe [Chippewa-Ojibway]), Maurice Kenny (Mohawk), Elizabeth Cook-Lynn (Crow Creek Sioux), Joseph Bruchac (Abenaki), Joy Harjo (Creek), Jimmie Durham (Wolf Clan Cherokee), Jim Barnes (Choctaw-Welsh), Carroll Arnett (Cherokee), Ray A. Youngbear (Mesquaki), Roberta Hill Whiteman (Oneida), Carter Revard (Osage), William Oandasan (Yuki), Peter Blue Cloud (Turtle Mohawk), Barney Bush (Shawnee-Cayuga), Jeanette Armstrong (Okanagon), Chrystos (Menominee), Robert Franklin Gish (Cherokee), Luci Tapahonso (Navajo), Duane Big Eagle (Osage), Haunani-Kay Trask (Hawaiian), Bobby Louise Bush (Chehalis), Thomas King (Cherokee), and others too numerous to mention. At the First North American Native Writers' Festival, held in July 1992, nearly one hundred Indian fiction and poetry writers appeared and read their work, participated on panels, and otherwise discussed the present and future of Native writing. In the context of the present discussion, I offer my interpretation of the following three Native writers in their connection to both the history of Indian writing and to the drive toward unique Indian identities.

LINDA HOGAN

"Uncle Sam was a cold uncle with a mean soul and a cruel spirit."

It remains the tragic irony of reservation Indians that the land they were "given" by the U.S. government is still largely controlled by government bureaucracy, especially when it comes to mineral, water, fishing, and grazing rights and tribal politics. As part of the Dawes Allotment Act of 1887, Indians then living on reservations were allotted 160 acres per person, but with the stipulation that the BIA and its agents in the field could determine both how the land was to be "developed" and whether or not any given Indian was "competent" to hold and manage his or her land. When oil was discovered in the Indian Territory that is now Oklahoma, in 1897, these stipulations gave way to a massive fraud perpetrated against the Osage, Apache, Choctaw, Chickasaw, Cherokee, Kiowa, Caddo, Seminole, and other Indian nations living there. Linda Hogan, a Chickasaw poet, essayist, and novelist, became familiar with this historical backdrop of her 1990 novel, *Mean Spirit*, through friends and family who had witnessed the cold-hearted, greedy manipulations of white entrepreneurs, Indian agents, lawyers, lawmen, and hired killers who dismantled entire Indian settlements in their pursuit of oil wealth. Her resultant novel, a final-four runner-up for the Pulitzer Prize in 1990, is an extraordinary and absorbing epic about those times (and their continuation up into the present) that touches as well on the deep humanism, trenchant dignity, and imaginative hopes of the Osage people who are its real subject. Her invocation of the land, reminiscent of Osage writer John Joseph Mathews's *Talking to the Moon* and of the Indians' relationship to it and all of nature, is resplendent with a magical realism and serendipitous beauty that make the historical tragedy of this book even more obscene.

As the title suggests, *Mean Spirit* is a work of spiritual juxtapositions played out in a historical context of cultures in collision. As Reverend Joe Billy says, "The Indian world is on a collision course with the white world."[23] Just as La Farge portrayed the infringement of white settlers in New Mexico and Arizona and their impact on Native culture, so Hogan takes the reader into the Oklahoma backcountry, where all hell is about to break loose. At the time of the novel (1922), many Osage had already become rich by leasing their land to white oilmen such as the incorrigible character John Hale, and Hogan's Indians, in the midst of such economic and cultural upheaval, are not a homogenous synonym for traditional lifeways, but rather unique Indian personalities at various distances on the path between tribalism and assimilation, or innocence and corruption. The mysterious Hill People, who live in the inchoate shamanistic magic of the past, are nonetheless linked spiritually with the young Nola Blanket, an oil-rich yet equally inchoate "modern" Indian girl traumatized by the murder of her mother, Grace, and subsequently lost in the fragile trappings of civilization. Belle and Moses Graycloud work their parcel of land by raising horses and beekeeping, while some of the younger Indians sport new cars, fancy American clothes, and "belong to the cash-paying Indians who were singing 'Amazing Grace' inside the church," some wearing paleface makeup or dyeing their hair blond with peroxide.[24] One can see such characters as these both spoofed and lauded in the work of artists Kevin Red Star, T. C. Cannon, and Fritz Scholder: Indians caught up in the gaudy material culture that they have made uniquely their own nonetheless. The rich diversity of Indian personages both mawkish and dignified, as defined by their clothing, their mannerisms, their actions, and ultimately their faith, pervades the novel and gives it both a real and a surreal atmosphere that is almost cinematic.

During the hot spell that opens the novel, for instance, many of the Indian characters have moved their beds outside, where Hogan conjures up one of many absurdist portraits:

> Belle Graycloud slept in the middle of her herb garden with a stubborn golden chicken roosting on the foot of the bed, a calico cat by the old woman's side, a fat spotted dog snoring on the ground, and a white horse standing as close to Belle as the fence permitted, looking at her with wide, reverent eyes.[25]

Michael Horse, an old "dreamer" who is beginning to doubt his prescience, is "the last person in Indian Territory to live in a tepee," and also the keeper of the "people's fire," which he never lets go out, carrying its coals from place to place as he has to.[26] The ghost of the old Indian John Stink, neither wholly incarnate nor wholly numinous, roams the countryside and town, cigar in hand, never sure whether he's alive or dead. Reminiscent of Gabriel Garcia Márquez's Macondo in *One Hundred Years of Solitude,* the Osage town of Watona is peopled with spirits and phenomena that delight the imagination and instill a sense of the mystery of life: the fortuneteller with no lines in her palm who sees the future but never returns to ordain it; the medicine corn that sprouts in a few days, as Horse learns "the languages of owls and bats"; the Catholic priest who "goes sane" and becomes an ascetic mystic living among the Indians like a latter-day St. Francis, blessing hogs and chickens; the old Indian who finally buys a new car that, along with dozens of brand-new bathtubs, finds its real use as a tomato hothouse—the novel is rife with brilliantly suggestive images forming a dreamscape that hints at what Horse knows: "There is not room enough, nor time, to search for the real story that lies beneath the rest."[27]

What we do learn of the "real story" is intriguing enough. By the final chapter, eight murders and one attempted murder of Osage people have occurred, all to secure ownership of the oil that lies beneath their ground, mapped out on a wall in the sheriff's office like a death constellation in the universe of the whites. The discordance between Euramerican and Indian cosmologies, and its resulting political ramifications, is made clear by several simple observations:

> "You know, Europeans have different constellations than we do." Belle was thinking of the sky, how where she saw a man and a woman standing together, the ones called sky and earth, they saw twin boys. And how where she saw two people holding one another, they saw a man and a weapon.[28]

Examining an iridescent star chart on the wall of his home, " 'They don't have a buffalo,' Moses said as he studied the map. 'No wonder we don't understand each other.' "[29] This disparity in spiritual mapmaking and in the cultural decipherment of natural signifiers is used by Hogan to enunciate the significant differences between white and Indian cultures and religious codes.

Another important example of this guiding theme of decipherment occurs at Sorrow Cave, the sacred medicine vortex of Osage life around Watona. The cave harbors thousands of bats, whose natural and symbolic essence is as "a race of people who stand in two worlds like we [Indians] do." As the Reverend Joe Billy and his wife, Martha, are venturing back to the abode of the Hill People, back to the "old ways," and hopefully out of harm's way, they come upon Sorrow Cave, and the narrator explains: "The ceiling was full of scratches made by bats who once lived there. It looked like an alphabet, a mysterious writing that wanted to be deciphered."[30] For the Osage, the cave holds the original medicine bundle of Joe Billy's father, one in which preserved bat carcasses come alive again as the people seek out the help of the bat medicine. In the larger context of Native shamanistic traditions, the cave can be seen as a portal into the supernatural world of vision-questing shamans who usually underwent altered states of consciousness, with the aid of peyote or native tobacco (*Datura inoxia* and its sister species). In most Indian cultures, the shamans would thus encounter their spirit helpers, usually bears or rattlesnakes among the Chumash and other far-western Native cultures, or, perhaps fictionally in this case, bats among the Osage. The shamans would then make petroglyphs or pictographs of these spirit helpers on the walls and ceilings of their sacred locales. Deep in Sorrow Cave, as well, is a ceremonial room, and

> [o]n the wall there were paintings [pictographs] of bats. Red bats. In a hallway there were blue fish, and more bats with red, opened wings, and the paintings of black buffalo. It was a sacred world they entered and everyone became silent and heard a distant dripping of water in the caveways, the echoing sounds, the breathing of earth.[31]

Hogan's Osage view of this locale and its attendant "scratches," or petroglyphs of bat markings and bat pictographs, indicates the cave and its bats as sacred entities and spirit helpers to the Hill People, progeny of the ancient ones. The cave is also symbolically referred to as "the mouth of Sorrow" that lay at the end of the Trail of Tears. To the white people of Watona, however, bats signify an antithetical, profane carrier of disease—namely rabies—to be hunted into extinction: "There was a one-dollar bounty per 'flying rat,' as the newspaper called them."[32] And by extension, the Indian people to whom they are sacred become a detested species as well.

This same dichotomy in cosmological symbology is played out with respect to eagles, hundreds of which are shot from the sky and shipped off to eastern taxidermists and roadside attractions; to Indian corpses robbed from their graves for archeological exhibits; and to the land itself, whose sacred identity as Mother Earth is profaned by overgrazing, oil drilling, and deforestation—the archetypes have "constellated" in vastly different ways for the two cultures. In this way, Hogan recognizes the psychic dynamics of interpretation and signification that have played so great a part in the demonization of Indian peoples and the ensuing desecrations they have endured.

So many historical atrocities come to life in *Mean Spirit* that the work becomes something of a textbook case of the sociopathology of the "pioneering spirit" of the American West. In direct correlation with the philosophical "misunderstandings" outlined above, political and legal horrors abound as well. Of two Indian boys sent away to Carlisle Indian School in Pennsylvania, one returns with his thumbs distended and useless from being hanged by them for trying to escape, and both return to lives of alcoholism and despair. The philosophy of the Carlisle School, promoted by its founder General Richard H. Pratt (formerly of Ft. Marion Prison, Florida), became a rallying cry for white educators and missionaries: "Kill the Indian, and save the man." Oftentimes such a fatuous distinction, as has been pointed out elsewhere, resulted in the killing or maiming of both. The treacheries of the legal system with regard to Indians, both nationally and locally, are well known; those perpetrated against the Osages in the novel underscore their inherent evil.

By 1923, "nearly all of the full-blood Indians were deemed incompetent by the court's competency commission. Mixed-bloods, who were considered competent, were already disqualified from receiving full payments [for their land leases] because of their white blood."[33] Even though the Osages had bought their land outright from the government, the BIA still reserved the right to manage its development, and within that context many pernicious opportunities arose. White men petitioned to marry Osage women who held claim to mineral or grazing rights—"The women were business invest-ments," writes Hogan; Indian agents forced their wards into bankruptcy; oil barons took out life insurance policies on Indians in lieu of collecting debts owed them, and then had the policies enacted prematurely through staged suicides and outright murders; in the novel, Nola Blanket, inheritor of her mother's oil-bearing land, is first sent to Watona Indian School, where she rebels, and is then assigned a white "guardian," who manages her legal and financial affairs into ruin. A half-breed sheriff's deputy, who becomes wise to the grim design of the archcriminal John Hale, is set up and ambushed. The tender-hearted horseman, Benoit, brother-in-law of the murdered Grace Blanket, is falsely charged with the death of his wife, Sara, but is conve-niently never brought to trial before he is found suspiciously hanged from the ceiling of his jail cell. In the end, the Osages of Watona, whose nature religion and bat magic are finally powerless against the morbid machina-tions and explosions of industry and ecocide, pack up and leave once again to another seemingly desolate locale. As Michael Horse writes in his ledger, "It was a fatal ignorance we had of our place; we did not know the ends to which the others would go to destroy us. We didn't know how much they were moved by the presence of money."[34]

Perhaps the most cogent part of the "real story" of *Mean Spirit* lies in the dilemma of how humanity should read the "book of nature," to use Descartes's phrase, in both its literal and allegorical senses. The essential differences between Indian and Euramerican readings of the natural world, including our human place in it, lie at the heart not only of Indian-Anglo relationships, but also of all human relationship with the phenomenal world. On the one hand, Christians worldwide have been commanded to "Be fruitful and multiply, and replenish the earth, and subdue it" (Genesis 1:28); Indian cultures, on the other, have traditionally tended to be subdued by nature, in the sense that they have come to terms with its animate power as both provider and destroyer. Christians, as Hogan points out repeatedly, have also come under the secular influence of the Cartesian notion that mind is separable and discrete from matter, a supposition that places both nature and the human body in the position of the Other, while the detached mind attains a level of determinant spiritual authority. As Horse, who is busy writing a new chapter to the Bible, points out to the Catholic priest cum ascetic:

> "For instance, where does [the Bible] say that all living things are equal?" The priest shook his head. " It doesn't say that. It says man has dominion over the creatures of the earth." "Well, that's where it needs to be fixed. That's part of the trouble, don't you see?"[35]

The transition from the scientific, technological, materialistic, and theological orthodoxies that have characterized Western thinking since Descartes, to the intuitive/magical, holistic, animistic, and revelatory practices that are characterized as Indian in Hogan's work, is one which most Indians writing today offer Western readers as a gift of their culture and a signifier of their Indian identities as deep ecologists and animist priests, formed through generations of existential experience. The questions posed in *Mean Spirit* about our disparate "readings" of the hieroglyphs of nature, and about the actions that follow from those readings, are certainly among the most important issues on the political and ecological forefronts today. America's common, though exceedingly cacophonous, search for a modern identity—whether religious, political, or economic—has not, until recently, taken seriously the profound cogency of what the "first Americans" have had to say about the environment and the book of nature at large. The Christian majority has repeatedly excluded them from the discourse. Even today, as Vine Deloria Jr. observes, "To listen to representatives of the Clinton administration, one would suspect that a large war party of Sioux Indians was waiting just beyond the beltway, ready to invade the District of Columbia and force members of the executive branch to participate in the Sun Dance."[36] Such has been the historical resistance of the westernized American psyche toward anything remotely serious about Indian culture, apart

from being applauded as an entertainment or copied as a form of disin-
genuous spirituality. Linda Hogan's work demands, given the matrix of
historical authenticity, that an Indian reading of the constellated archetypes
of nature and self be given very serious consideration.

SHERMAN ALEXIE

Poetry = Anger x Imagination
Lester FallsApart

In late 1994, I had an opportunity to talk with the ascending Spokane-Cœur
d'Alene writer Sherman Alexie, who by age thirty in 1996 had five books of
poetry, two collections of short stories, and two novels in print. We talked
about the reliability of certain Indian and "wannabe" Indian activist writers
and critics. In reading Alexie's work, it had become painfully clear to me that
he was very keen to distinguish between "authentic" and inauthentic information on modern Indian life on every level, including the blood quantum
and tribal affiliations of those writers claiming to speak authoritatively on
Indian issues. "The worst thing about him," Alexie was saying about one of
the people in question, "is his homophobia." I thought it peculiar that this
obviously heterosexual Indian man with a mind full of other issues would be
concerned about a subject so seemingly unrelated to Indian affairs, but he
went on to explain that, while this noted writer had insisted that there had
never been "gay" Indians in any tribe, Alexie knew differently; traditionally,
he said, there had always been, at least among his tribes, androgynous,
bisexual, or homosexual people who were known as "two-spirited" and who
were generally given important shamanic roles within the tribe. This is
borne out in early research by such ethnologists as Ruth Underhill, who
found among the Navajo such persons, called by the French anthropological
term "berdaches, those males who led a woman's life."[37] Such concern for
detail, often at odds with stereotype, rumor, and myth mongering, is a
hallmark of Alexie's writing as well, in which he denounces much of the
Noble Savage/Ignoble Savage categorization of white-authored Indian identities and writes from his own experience, often with highly comical as well
as vengefully plangent effect. In *Reservation Blues* (1995), his first novel, these
qualities vie for the reader's attention and ultimately conjoin in a portrait of
Indian lives that is itself a search for identity and survival among the charred
cinematic remains of modern reservation life.

Acutely aware of all the preexisting stereotypical identities that have been the bane of modern Indian life, Alexie skillfully weaves many of them into the context of this picaresque tale of an all-Indian rock-and-roll band whose brief flirtation with fame catalyzes his characters' fates, all within the larger contexts of history and of nonlinear time. Like the work of the Indian artists discussed in chapter 8, *Reservation Blues* howls with an intrepid anger against the cruelties of the past, while at the same time illustrating how there is still much to confront among the cruelties of the present.

In the stroboscopic time evoked by the author, seemingly encoded in the DNA of all Indians living and dead, events of 134 years ago replay in the present like a seamless memory, a life lived on a Möbius strip of undulating and vanishing surfaces. Big Mom, the spiritual elder of the Spokane Indian Reservation in Wellpinit, Washington, resides in this nonlinear time. She witnessed the massacre of most of her tribe in 1861 at the hands of Colonel George Wright's mounted 9th Cavalry, "heard the first gunshot, which reverberated in her DNA," but in the present of the novel she still lives up on Wellpinit Mountain, guiding the lives of musicians with the simple reminder that "music created and re-created the world daily."[38] George Wright, who died in 1865, reappears as a record company executive who re-cruits the Indian band for Cavalry Records. The famous black blues guitarist Robert Johnson, who died mysteriously in 1938, also resides in this con-tinuum, appearing just as mysteriously on the Spokane Reservation in 1992 as an instrument of "[t]hose blues [that] were ancient, aboriginal, indige-nous."[39] Throughout the novel, "That colt [shot between the eyes in 1861 by Wright] fell to the grass of the clearing, to the sidewalk outside a reservation tavern, to the cold, hard coroner's table in a Veteran's Hospital."[40] Like a film loop made from old cowboy and Indian shoot-'em-up movies, the horrors and the stereotypes keep popping up on all fronts. Alexie realizes both the angst and the absurd humor of such a hallucinatory time. That things have not changed much since the original creation of the reservation system is the most poignant and pointed refrain, oftentimes sung against a background of laughter that one reviewer has called "gallows humor," which in turn is a saving grace among many modern Indian writers.

Central to the themes of dislocation, desperation, and dissipation that haunt *Reservation Blues* is also the effect of Christianity, both in the past and the present, on Indian peoples. Here Alexie maintains an admirable equi-librium, neither wholly contemptuous nor wholly valorizing of white reli-gion (now a significant part of the lives of the many Christianized Indians).

Father Arnold, of the Wellpinit Catholic Church, is a rightfully conflicted priest, administering as best he can to the people that his avowed religion attempted to deracinate and Christianize only a century or two before. In his naiveté, one hears both the sincerity and the ignorance of the missionary mind "at play in the fields of the Lord." When he first arrives at the reservation, the narrator tells us, his "Indian education was quick and brutal": he had come "expecting tipis and buffalo," only to be informed that "it was those dang Sioux Indians," the movie and television stereotype—"Those Sioux," a tribal elder explains, "always get to be on television. They get everything."[41] Father Arnold stays on until he can no longer bear either his love for an Indian girl or the seeming senselessness of his mission, and Alexie finds in him "a good white man" who, despite the often heinous history of his order, can offer human love to his congregation, at least for a while.[42]

Other aspects of Christian influence are not treated with the same magnanimity, however. The sheer hypocrisy of Father Arnold's bishop calls forth another, more indignant, voice in the novel. When the bishop intones to the faltering Arnold, "I know it's never easy ministering to such a people as the Indians. They are a lost people, God knows," we sense Alexie's irony and the anger of the betrayed. In the chapter "My God Has Dark Skin," the horror of the Conquest reverberates in the song lyrics that introduce the chapter, composed by Alexie and Colville Indian Jim Boyd:

> My braids were cut off in the name of Jesus
> To make me look so white
> My tongue was cut out in the name of Jesus
> So I would not speak what's right
> My heart was cut out in the name of Jesus
> So I would not try to feel
> My eyes were cut out in the name of Jesus
> So I could not see what's real
> And I've got news for you
> But I'm not sure where to begin
> Yeah, I've got news for you
> My God has dark skin
> My God has dark skin
> I had my braids cut off by black robes
> But I know they'll grow again

I had my tongue cut out by these black robes
But I know I'll speak 'til the end
I had my heart cut out by the black robes
But I know what I still feel
I had my eyes cut out by black robes
But I know I see what's real.[43]

The experiences of another character, Victor Joseph, also point out the dark side of Christian influence. Shuffled off to the mission school for a summer, Victor is the object of a pedophile priest's indecent affections. " 'It's a shame we had to cut your hair,' the priest said. 'You are such a beautiful boy' "—and this just before the priest "kissed Victor full and hard on the mouth."[44] In light of these condemning sentiments and incidents, which echo throughout the book, it is indeed charitable of the narrator to provide Father Arnold with the grace to tell a young Indian parishioner, who laments her inability to "be just like one of those white girls," that "Jesus was Jewish. He probably had dark skin and hair."[45]

Also relevant to this discussion is what Alexie makes of his "medicine woman" character, Big Mom. While in many ways she symbolizes the traditional, communal aspects of tribal religion, mysticism, and magic, her character also veers importantly away from New Age, mostly romanticized white versions of that tradition: "A concussion," one character points out to a wannabe Indian, "is just as traditional as a sweatlodge."[46] The concatenations and ambiguities in her own and other characters' personal identities belie any varnished stereotypes that readers might wish for in Indian literature. At once a mysterious old sage living up on the cloud-shrouded mountain, where only "the called" are allowed to visit, and the best fry bread cook on the reservation, Big Mom is also the secret teacher of music for everyone from Elvis Presley to the Andrews Sisters, and the healer of maimed and miserable Robert Johnson, who stays at her cabin. Alexie manages to impart through her his underlying faith in Indian sacramentalism and simultaneously to undermine any false piousness such as that invoked by Helen Hunt Jackson in her characterizations of Father Salvierderra or Ramona herself. " 'She's just a part of God,' " as Thomas Builds-the-Fire, the author's alter ego and protagonist, says. "We're all part of God, enit? Big Mom is just a bigger part of God."[47] (The word *enit* is Indian vernacular for "isn't it," part of the idiosyncratic Indian English that flavors Alexie's writing with a modern twang.) Alexie's treatment of Big Mom serves as an earnest demystification of Noble Savage types through a humanization of her essential ambiguity. A healer, a "musical genius," and a clairvoyant, she is also a practitioner of common sense and mistress of the obvious. Humor and magic are held in an archetypal tension that allows a sense of the real, even the mundane, to deconstruct lofty or sentimentalized expectations. One of the novel's finest moments has Big Mom enacting a seriocomic parody of the Christian parable of the loaves and fishes, in which she divulges her "secret": " 'Mathematics,' Big Mom said."[48]

With this unsettling combination of mythos and monstrosity, "blasphemy" and ardor, sacred and profane, Alexie brings to life idiosyncratic Indian characters whose identities are formed in the crucible of fate and free will, and who emerge from their personal histories as three-dimensional characters acting on the moving stage of time. They are not the idealized Indians wished for by the New Age groupies Betty and Veronica, for instance, who "think Indians got all the answers."[49] These two New Age seekers, carrying all the stereotypical baggage of the Noble Savage, run into the all-Indian rock-and-roll band, Coyote Springs, early on and raise hell with two of the rowdier band members, Victor Joseph and Junior Polatkin. " 'White people want to be Indians,' " says Betty, " 'You all have things we don't have. You live at peace with the earth. You are so wise.' "[50] Along the way, they learn the downside of being an Indian, much to their chagrin and disillusionment. But that is the point that Alexie strives to make, time and time again: Why would anyone *want* to be an Indian in contemporary America, given the degraded survival and racism that most modern Indians are heir to? Alexie warns anyone who might think of Indians in such fatuous terms as Betty does, that you have to see "everything," as Robert Johnson, and the reader, also learn. Those who do not, such as Veronica and Betty, bastardize and further trivialize Indian culture, as exemplified by the fact that these white girls end up posing as Indians to become recording stars, instead of the real Indians of Coyote Springs—manipulated again by the corporate image mongers of white America. The "everything" that Alexie invokes is at the vortex of *Reservation Blues*.

The reservation paradigm of Alexie, like that of Linda Hogan, among others, is not often instilled with the comforting sweetness and primordial profundity that authors such as Helen Hunt Jackson and Oliver LaFarge are inclined to favor. Certainly not the Red Atlantis of John Collier, reservation life in these authors' eyes is one of destitution and catastrophic depression. If one might invoke Blake's proverb that "excess of sorrow laughs," Alexie's reservation Indians are continually on the edge of that excess, finally laughing because "there was nothing else left to do."[51] Some of Alexie's stories and characters drift from book to book—they are piteous refrains or soaring anthems that cycle through all of his work and make it whole. This repetition is reflective of traditional Indian storytelling as well, in which tales are told and retold throughout the decades, embellished and changed as circumstances warrant. The kids are left alone in the car on a cold night while mom and dad drink themselves into the oblivion of last call at the Powwow Tavern; Thomas Builds-the-Fire helps Victor scatter his father's ashes at Spokane Falls, like seeds for a new harvest of salmon in the dead river; Indians sit along a roadway or on a decaying piece of storefront sidewalk, sharing a bottle of wine and a can of commodity food; drunken Indians, "so many drunks on the reservation, so many," are frequently seen passing out in dumpsters or running their beat-up cars into telephone poles ("Car wrecks are an Olympic sport for you Indians," jokes the reservation doctor); somebody's father burns all the furniture out in the front lawn on New Year's Eve, and in the next telling, he burns down the whole damn house; the pony who is also Thomas Builds-the-Fire in a previous story is the same one shot by Colonel Wright in *Reservation Blues*.[52] With every iteration and reiteration, new contexts emerge to create new meanings, new identities, that form a Heraclitean enantiodromia (or drama of opposites) that, to recall Jung, is engaged in "a rhythm of negative and positive, loss and gain, dark and light" common to fairy tales, folk tales, and the rest of significant literature, and essential to individuation and human authenticity.[53]

We must not overlook what is positive, gainful, and light in Alexie's work. If the indignities, horrors, and strife of reservation life provide the crucible for survival and individuation, as well as for failure and death, then his self-effacing humor, the power of his writing, and his diligent compassion are the proof of a certain transformation, however tenuous it may be, even by his own admission. Alexie is a recovering alcoholic, a fact that is the subject of some of his earlier work, and he knows full well how prodigious a struggle that can be. As he writes in "The Alcohol Love Poems," "Alcohol is a drum / calling me. Alcohol//calls me. Sometimes / it's so hard//not to hear / that drum. Sometimes//it's so hard / not to dance."[54] Many of Alexie's characters—Lester, Victor, Junior, and others—are heirs to the curse of alcoholism, sometimes fatally so. Like Father Arnold, the reader wonders, "What did [Indians] have to laugh about? Poverty, suicide, alcoholism?"[55] One feels, in reading much of Alexie's work, that vertiginous uncertainty about identity that also informs the work of Hachivi Edgar Heap of Birds, but humor almost always grounds us, at least momentarily, in the realm of human pathos, for humor often springs from that excess of sorrow, and often seems both its cure and its clarification.

While many white and Indian readers may protest the incantatory depression that also looms in Alexie's work, as a literary mood it has all the significance it carries for an Eliot or a Steinbeck, a Bob Dylan or a Woody Guthrie, for whom also the "grapes of wrath" have inspired an essential wisdom and literary wit. As fellow poet Adrian C. Louis (Lovelock Paiute) has said in earnest praise of Alexie:

> He speaks to people in hopes of bringing about change; he speaks as a functioning ear and eye of the people; he speaks as a seer. Alexie is not writing the intellectualized masturbation that passes for so much of today's poetry. He is a singer, a shaman, a healer . . .[56]

SIMON J. ORTIZ: REINTERPRETING THE ROSEBUD

Within days of the 1890 massacre at Wounded Knee, South Dakota, U.S. Cavalry personnel, including photographers, returned to the frozen scene to cart off the bodies of some three hundred men, women, and children of the Minneconjous (Hunkpapa Sioux). The photographs survive today, some showing corpses of the hundred or so who died, not from bullets but from the bitter cold, in various gestures of final rigor: hands grasping upward, bodies in their last spasm of escape. A hundred years later, Acoma Pueblo poet Simon J. Ortiz spent a winter reexamining this same ground as a teacher on the Rosebud Sioux Indian Reservation, reflecting on the continued survival of those known as the Plains Indians in an environment still threatening, still plagued with the effects of a tragic Indian policy, but still somehow, in Ortiz's heart, the vital homeland of a strong and resilient people. His themes in *After and Before the Lightning* (1993) articulate the fact that, while the cavalry of 1890 left a wake of despair and destruction in the prairie winter, the Lakota of the Rosebud "know the sacred beauty of the . . . homeland which they regard with wonder and awe."[57] Ortiz's personal journey into the Dis-like hell of a Lakota winter finds it full of both sublime terror and a regenerative humility that seem primordial resonances of how

Indian peoples might always have adapted to a nature, and now a history, that have been the crucible of their survival.

On first reading, Ortiz's work in *Lightning* seems almost banal in its diarial formality. Poems intercut with short prose passages describe the minutiae of his daily existence, an inner life delicately but deliberately respondent to the overbearing whims of prairie nature. He and his students and colleagues are often on the road in an ice storm, in a car with no heater; the rancher next door seems eternally at work against the elements, keeping his horses and cattle from succumbing to the incessant cold; there is never enough wood in the firebox to warm the walls of his room, and when it is gone there is none even to steal; the quotidian moment, ever so quietly or so violently, is often the object of attention. But in another moment's recognition, one senses all the mundane news of the world collapsing or exploding into a phenomenal continuum of profound insights touching the racial memory. "The Right Instinct," for example, opens with a typical setting out on the road that "could go anywhere, nowhere. / The ridge was clear, road blown clear"; while we are aware at first of "Nothing / but the wind and snowdrifts claiming the road," a miasma of whiteout and winter, the connection is soon made to "a glacial planet in a deathly white galaxy," and to the "everything" of the poet's "nerves of my body / and quickening mind." "It doesn't take much more than a mile / to figure it out," is the clever observation about both the poet's own style and its subtle reflexiveness. "My imagination / is a safety net." Simultaneously, both the macrocosm and the microcosm are revealed in a lone man standing at the side of a windblown road in the middle of nowhere. We might wonder, knowing the poet's origins, if the "deathly white galaxy" is a metaphor for white civilization that seems to have swallowed up any direction or destination an Indian might set out for. The stark simplicity of pastoral surface cracks a bit to reveal a crucial existential moment: to proceed or turn back on the long road to destiny? "Turn back," the poet urges, for "Nothing is certain / but the instinct for safety and survival."[58] There are many other moments held in these poems when the answer is reversed, and "there are people walking along the highway. / One footstep after another, hoping for distance, / a necessary place that is destination" (from "Destination: Destiny").[59] For Ortiz, speaking from an identity that "know[s] what it's like leaving things behind," survival is an interior dialogue between ambivalence and wisdom, based on the experience of his people:

Everything is so huge, dimensions so vast
there is no need to seek significance.
A silver glow tilts the prairie hills
toward the impossibly held balance
we have never easily been able to achieve.
(from "Destination, Seeking")[60]

The urge to "seek significance," in a Western philosophical and psychological sense, is also that which seeks determinant answers, a final solution to
the questions of existence. From a linguistic point of view, such significance
ultimately empowers the dominant religions of the world—Christianity,
Islam, etc.—if it is held in stasis as dogma and universal truth. Ortiz, reflecting an essentially Indian way of thinking that avoids such linearity and
absolutism, brings to bear an acausal and extemporaneous notion of the
imbued magic of living that is the dialectical opposite of rational Western
thinking. Ortiz's magic, consciously resisting the grandiosity of Western
spirituality, derives from a certain way of perceiving the real that, like the
illustration above, includes the microcosmic and the macrocosmic in the
same moment: a sort of eternal now. As in his poems "Magic Always" and
"More Real Magic," this resistance is both eloquent and country simple.
"Red fire on the grate, / magic idea, / the cosmos and cell / enjoined, /
perfection not sought/but there," offer the first lines of "Magic Always."
Such a notion is as old as Western philosophy itself; the early Greek Hera-
clitus remarked, on looking into his fire, that "there are gods even here."
Yet such ordinary metaphysics have largely been lost in their translation
into Christian theology, with its emphases on grand ideas, the preference for
an afterlife, and priestly mediation between the beholder and the beheld.
"We're only human," Ortiz states simply, "fervent and eager, / tricks for
magic / in our fingers."[61] Putting the lie to Eurocentric ideas about the
complex mysticism of Native spirituality, Ortiz's "More Real Magic" enjoins
again in one lucid poem the natural and the supernatural, inseparable in
traditional aboriginal thought:

Sunlit pine
snow falls
from a branch
one motion one time
magic one time

Soundless
one time falling
snow one time
for me is magic

Could not have
looked in time
to see it
magic real is that

Light touches
me snow pine
motion and magic
together in time

Prairie sun
and snow touch
reality more
than this moment

Single pine branch
won't break
one time ever
always bend always

Not alone but one
all things in one
snow pine light one
me motion magic one.[62]

Similar in formal construction to Hachivi Edgar Heap of Birds's installation piece or Dickinson's poem #216, discussed previously, this poem achieves a prelinguistic profundity by virtue of its very paucity of language. Built principally of simple nouns, it demonstrates how significance (and magic) is but the momentary occurrence of random things coming together, requiring only the perceptive eye of the beholder, and the beholder's art, to render a plethora of meanings that resound together instantly, only to disappear. "The future is secured without the construction of certainty," seems the antinomian message.[63] The modernist form used here—sparse, open, reductive—is as deliberate as its message is archaic, both implying a preverbal experience of the archetypal unity of nature, human-kind, and supernature.

Reinforcing Ortiz's conceptions of survival and magic are those of "process" and "margins." Bound together in an aesthetic of "belief, art, ingenuity, concept, and, most of all, prayer and respect," the "holy fit" of Ortiz's poetry emphasizes survival as a process undertaken in the ordinary world and understood and communicated both in the margins of ourselves that we share with others and in the marginal world that Indians now occupy.[64] The sacred appears, for Ortiz, in the mindful activities of the living, as when a neighboring white man, sensitive to Native traditions, places a piece of sage in each of the joints of his new house's frame. The essential nature of the cosmos and the interlocking human world are noted in the mindfulness of process, not the concretization of tradition but its timely applications in "motion and change."[65] As Andrew Wiget has noted, "What Ortiz hopes for and believes in is an ideology of work which would see labor not as an opportunity for exploitation but as the occasion for renewing creative integration of relationships."[66]

While very much a traditionalist at heart, Ortiz makes it clear that tradition is not a dead language but a living utility, adapting itself continually to changing environments, both natural and human. Several of the poems in this collection, for example, use traditional Indian words and songs translated into an English idiom to invoke a sense of tradition; they are not meant to mystify the poems, or to demand that the reader be familiar with the Lakota or Navajo or Acoma languages, but to recognize the historical and cultural matrix of the poems and their antecedents in prehistory. Like the traditional forms incorporated by some Indian studio artists such as Jaune Quick-to-See Smith and Diego Romero, they appear as identity markers and signifiers of the Indianness of the message being evoked. They are also part of the process whereby Indian feelings and perceptions are translated into English poetry, a process inclusive of prayer and ancient songs. Buffalo, Coyote, and the Snow Shiwana (winter spirits) appear in *Lightning* not as icons of the past but as metaphors for a living landscape and mindscape that are open to all potentialities, even humorous ones; perhaps especially humorous ones, as in this story of a modern Antelope Father-Elder seeking the Snow Shiwana:

As Antelope Father-Elder, he'd go in one of the four directions.
"Haaweh-shthih Shiwana, I'll sing you a song, I who is the Ante-

lope Elder," he said. And he sang for the Snow Shiwana, the spirits of winter. His song was: Hahdhi-shra Haawehshthih Shiwana?
Hahdhi-shra Haaweh-shthih Shiwana? . . . Well, later on, telling
about that morning, he would say, "As I was singing to all the
directions, looking all around at the Haaweh-shthih clouds, suddenly I fell into one of those frozen water holes covered with
snow!

" 'Right here I am, the Shiwana,' the Shiwana said to me. 'Now
you've found me.' "[67]

As Waters has noted about the Hopi way, this little story incorporates a
sophisticated mix of the sacred and the profane, the cosmic and the banal, to
invoke a human seriocomedy that is delightfully provocative. The arch
seriousness of biblical grandiosity is nowhere to be found. Instead, we find a
calmingly humorous story of the serendipitous nature of human experience
vis-à-vis the gods, reminiscent of early Germanic fairy tales and other international folklore. The Trickster, an archetypal figure in much traditional
literature, emerges here to resonate with the same spirit of chance, change,
and synchronicity. Indeed, the Trickster, often portrayed as Coyote, perme-
ates Native American folklore and creation stories.

Similarly, the invocation of the Buffalo spirit Muushaitrah in "Buffalo
Light Now" incorporates an Acoma song that, in the succeeding stanza, is
translated into English so as to include all readers in the dream of fruition
and plenty that the song implores. And Coyote, so often today a commer-
cialized ideogram meant to signify Indianness, is herein "Right before us . . .
We look at each other, unbelieving at first, and then back to Coyote crossing
the road. Right there in front of us, heading north. It is real and actual, the
truth of Existence within the strangely beautiful vastness of this prairie. We
know we are alive."[68] Thus, trite icons of Indian life are renewed in the
sacred moment of the present, in an experiential context that avoids mystification and instead examines the process of seeing the sacred in the "Common Trials: Every Day," as one section is entitled.

Coyote as a Trickster figure is perhaps the most salient example of how
Indian writers feel about and utilize the shape-shifting ambiguity of the
archetypes; Ortiz, as Paula Gunn Allen has observed, "delights in discov-
ering Coyote multitudinously reincarnated, rattling off his slick stories,
making deals in barrooms and Greyhound bus stations, fooling and being

fooled, and somehow, like the spirit of the peoples he embodies, still beautifully surviving."[69] People who are subject to stereotyping and pigeonholing necessarily embrace identities that are complex, transformative, and elusive. As Wong points out, "The Navajo emphasis on dynamic processes would certainly include a sense of self that embodies the 'concept of motion,' a self that is continually shifting, changing, going."[70]

While the "deathly white galaxy" of "The Right Instinct" may or may not be a reference to encroaching white civilization, it is clear elsewhere in *Lightning* that Ortiz does not wish to skirt the real social tragedies that encumber Indian peoples today. Indeed, they are as much an embedded part of his existence as are the winter spirits or the Buffalo song. "As an Acoma Indian in the Americas," he writes in his introduction, "the dreaded reality of despair, death, and loss because of oppressive colonialism has been too often present, and I cannot deny that. No one can, certainly no one who understands and has undergone debilitating colonialization. My personal experience and history have been burdened with too much of that."[71] "Loss and loss will stalk us," intone the last lines of "Loss and Grief Finding Us," "finding us too soon and there could be the tremor / across everything. But we will hold and hold." The instability of Indian reservation life, largely due to the vicissitudes of government policy even today, when the BIA finds itself fighting in Congress to maintain an adequate budget for Indian people, is poignantly realized by Ortiz, an unrestrained elegist as well as an uncanny, existential pastoralist. "Yesterday, the slightest tremor / could have avalanched even the prairie," are the opening lines of this foreboding poem that laments a trio of suicides. Gunshots ring out at the funeral of a "sister, poet"; an Indian farmer "pull[s] the trigger in broad daylight, law and God standing by." What could be worse, the poet asks, than for the survivors to feel the rankle that "our rational and bearable humanity is a common error"?[72] Such is the numbing, often left unspoken, despair of those who have experienced a suicide, whose emotional residue is perhaps the most difficult of all grief to articulate, to rationalize, and to overcome. Is to live by the rules of survival in this world a "common error"? Is it by some margin an act of cowardice to find or make life "bearable"? These destabilizing questions haunt Indian life and literature precisely because they are unavoidable; most Indians living in the United States today do so under the burden of so-called Third World conditions of dire poverty, landlessness, rampant malnutrition and diabetes, low educational attainment, high unemployment, and a pervasive incidence of death by exposure, tuberculosis, fetal alcohol syndrome, infant mortality, plague, and similar maladies.[73] Suicide is not uncommon; it is but a symptom of the larger humiliation and degradation that Indian people experience every day.

Although some Indian scholars and intellectuals feel that social realism and political observation do not tell the whole story about current Indian affairs, as Ortiz observes, most Indians who have lived through it cannot deny it. "When you're cold and hungry," Ortiz says, reflecting on the lives of his parents,

> when you need things, you do what you can, yes do what you can. Sometimes you do even the necessary thing you don't want to do: go to the government office, stand in line, wait your turn, cry inside, tighten your face, wait, be insulted, pretend it doesn't matter, pretend it's not that cold and you're not that hungry.
>
> Watching the blue jay and pheasants, I think of my parents so fierce with their courage and determination to be free. Watching the blue jay and the pheasants, I think too of how people are driven to slavery in today's world.[74]

Like Linda Hogan and Sherman Alexie, Ortiz understands and does not accept the deprivations of his people. Knowing his own history, he is keenly aware of the anger that it provokes today among the living inheritors of this corrupt history of colonialism. "Despair or anger?" he asks. "It's an unfair question. I know what the people feel. Helplessness." "When it is enough," he asks further, "will it happen?"[75] Here he is referring, bluntly enough, to the potential for armed struggle for the basic rights guaranteed to Indians as sovereign nations by treaty so many years ago, and as yet unrealized, or worse, perpetually abrogated.

conclusion

10

> My earlier series . . . Coyote gave me a chance to confront the world, and the
> Stone Poems are giving me a chance to confront myself in a new world. It is a
> world where blacks and whites are slowly, very slowly, turning into grays—grays
> with all the shades of uncertainty, fear, growth, and wonder.
>
> *Henry Fonseca, Maidu artist*

Henry Fonseca, a widely popular and often imitated artist, seems to suggest
that in the world of the modern Indian, issues of identity are becoming more
flexible and less and less dependent on the bipolar opposition between black
and white, or between white and red. The stereotypical sameness of the "red
man" as constructed by the racist ideology of white America appears to be
giving way to new dimensions of Indian authenticity, as more and more
Indians seek to rediscover their human complexities and potentialities and
to redefine their identities in order to continue to live *as Indians*. Recognizing the perilous prospects of total assimilation into the white hegemony,
modern Indians have insisted, for instance, on the teaching of their native
languages in reservation schools and are busily trying to recapitulate their
traditional religions and customs in a process that Vine Deloria Jr. calls
"retribalization." The repatriation of artifacts and bones from museum collections back to ancestral burial grounds is at last taking place, as is the
return of other items deemed sacred by Indian petitioners. All across Indian
Country, varying amplitudes of resistance continue to assail both historical
inequities and present insults.

The very language that embodies Indian stereotype is itself on trial in the
national media, as Indian activists condemn, for instance, the naming of

sports teams after English-borne epithets for Native Americans, such as the Atlanta Braves, the Kansas City Chiefs, and the Cleveland Indians, all of which amount, in the thinking of Indians, to naming such teams the Kikes, the Niggers, or the Nips. Indian writers, artists, and activists on all fronts are sure to condemn all the noxious stereotypes discussed herein, while at the same time initiating an internecine conceptual battle about the nature of each other's Indianness.

Coincidentally, many are also seeking the power of a Euramerican education, knowing that they, too, must learn the socioeconomic ways of the white culture that surrounds them, if they are to remain economically viable. One of the potentially most vital instruments of Indian survival into the twenty-first century is the formation of the American Indian College Fund and its twenty-nine member schools, all based on or near reservations across the United States. Amidst sometimes scurrilous tribal politics and the vicissitudes of the BIA, tribal colleges offer sanctuaries of intellectual and political freedom, as well as a foundational education in both Native traditions and modern liberal arts and sciences curricula. The combination seeks to imbue Indian students with a spirit of authentic self-worth and the ability to translate that value into a viable lifestyle on or off the reservation. As students and teachers, Indians both here and in the mainstream are also creating a new subtext of cultural pluralism and a reawakening of Native philosophies and lifeways within the heretofore white-dominated curricula. Many work off-reservation in the polyglot mainstream of U.S. society, while living on the reservation or at least returning to it frequently for rejuvenation within their own traditions. Many Indians, like many non-Indians, are just awakening to the dignity and identifying histories of their traditional cultures, having long been under the illusion that they had no meaningful spiritual or intellectual heritage. The environment of the tribal college campus has made creativity and dialogue attractive alternatives to self-destructive suffering and polemical rage; it has already turned many a young Indian mind toward a more individuated approach to life in the modern world.

Indians are also relearning political activism, as the Indian occupation of Alcatraz Island in 1969 and the standoff at Wounded Knee, South Dakota, in 1973 have demonstrated. The "Red Power" movement of the 1960s and 1970s took up the causes of Indian civil rights and political sovereignty, and Indian lawyers have argued numerous Native land claims in state and federal courts nationwide, seeking tribal autonomy from non-Indian governments and guarantees to their treated land holdings. As Phillip J. Deloria notes:

> An obsessive awareness of politics came to permeate many tribes, spanning all levels from the local to the federal. Although political maneuvering often created dissension within tribes, many of its more skilled participants were also able to help their people in significant ways through social and economic programs.[1]

The American Indian Movement, founded in 1968, and the Native American Rights Fund (1970 to the present) have grown to national prominence as defenders of Indian legal and civil rights.

Recent developments suggest that the BIA, the Department of the Interior, and the U.S. Treasury have, over the last several decades, mismanaged and actually "lost" or misappropriated unspecified millions of dollars (up to $2.4 billion) of Indian monies funneled through their offices. The Native American Rights Fund filed suit against the federal government in the spring of 1996, alleging "illegal conduct in what is viewed as the largest and most shameful financial scandal ever involving the United States government."[2] As of 1996, Indians throughout the country still live under the sway of such contradictory and debilitating BIA policies, much as they have since the inception of the agency. Neither fully sovereign nations nor fully entitled wards of the state, Indian societies exist in a power vacuum arbitrated by the authority of the federal government. This vacuum has necessitated innovative Indian approaches to treating their own ills, which today, as much as ever, threaten their continued survival. Despair, poverty, alcoholism ("17.0 percent to 19.0 percent of all Indian deaths are probably alcohol-related," as compared with the general U.S. average of 4.7 percent[3]), fetal alcohol syndrome, suicide, fractious tribal governments, AIDS, diabetes, land and resource management, tribal gaming operations, and other problematic situations are increasingly being addressed within Indian communities themselves, without the intervention of the federal government. Each success brings tribes closer to sovereignty and closer to each other, as intertribal solutions are being worked out in increasing numbers.

While Indians attempt to disavail themselves of their reliance on government assistance, the U.S. Congress has increasingly, and prematurely, cut funds to Indian social services budgets under the Carter, Reagan, Bush, and

Clinton administrations. Despite protestations from the BIA itself and the Department of the Interior under Bruce Babbitt, the 1995 Congress slashed the president's 1996 budget for the BIA by $434.5 million, 15 percent below the level of 1995. Tribal priority allocations were cut by $220 million, "which will result in Tribes losing 35 percent of their funds needed to support critical programs at the local tribal level." Funding for school tuition and new school construction on BIA-managed reservations, as well as funding for BIA staff at their Washington and Albuquerque offices, were also severely cut (so much so that the bureau predicted the termination of almost all staff in these offices).[4] "I look at this budget and get very angry because essentially what we're dealing with is the integrity and honesty of the United States Government," commented Richard Brannan of the Wind River Reservation in Wyoming.[5] Navajo Nation President Albert Hale "argued that Indians had relinquished their lands in return for treaties with the U.S. government that bound the federal government to provide for Indians' basic needs. [This is] the worst attack on Indians in 100 years."[6] In addition, "an increasingly conservative judiciary offered extremely narrow interpretations of Indian rights both under treaties and under the U.S. Constitution." The question of Indian religious autonomy has also recently come under new restrictions, and "Native American [religious] traditions were [once again] considered too controversial" to merit full protection under the American Indian Religious Freedom Act of 1978.[7]

Lacking any credible resolution of the ambiguities inherent in Indian sovereignty at the end of the twentieth century, Washington bureaucrats tend to blow with the prevailing winds from administration to administration, further eroding the stability of individual Indian economies and the hope for any accountable national attitude toward Indian Country. In his 1996 work entitled *Killing the White Man's Indian*, Fergus M. Bordewich has suggested, and plausibly so, the necessity of an amendment to the U.S. Constitution that would define once and for all time the status of Indians, and especially reservation Indians and Indian Nations, with respect to the legal framework of the American government.[8]

The aura of incipient racism and mythological tyranny noticed by Waters among the Hopi also continues to plague Indian identities. Two recent events highlight the persistence of racially motivated discrimination, even among Indians themselves. The first concerns the formulation and passage of Public Law 101–644 under the Bush administration, in 1990. The law, also called the Indian Arts and Crafts Act (IACA), like its predecessor of 1935 (the Indian Arts and Crafts Board), ostensibly seeks to protect Indian artists and craftspersons from non-Indian copyists and imitators. The law requires, however, that Indian artists prove their affiliation with an Indian tribe, either by documenting their blood quantum ("Indian" artists must be "one quarter or more of Indian blood by birth") or by being registered as tribal members in the national registry of sanctioned Indian tribes, begun in the 1880s. The problems with this law are threefold.

First, since the inception of the national Indian tribal registry, many Indians have refused or otherwise been denied inclusion on the official list, because their tribes were not recognized as such by government criteria. The progeny of these Indians today, whether or not they are full-blooded or even quarter-blooded Indians, have no way of officially proving their heritage, since their maternal or paternal lineages are not recorded. Second, as Patricia Limerick and others point out, the likelihood of any full-blooded Indians existing at all after circa the year 2080 is extremely unlikely (by 1990, the proportion had shrunk to about 20 percent due to intermarriage between Indians and other races). That Indian artists must be of provable blood quantum to sell their work as "Indian art" has already had serious ramifications among collectors who purchased art before 1990; museums such as the Denver Art Museum, while trying to collect and show important Indian art, are permitted to exhibit only those artists approved under the IACA; and Indian artists heretofore exhibiting and selling their work are now required to have the "pure Indian" seal of approval. As postmodern Cherokee artist Jimmie Durham has announced in an "Artist's Disclaimer" that accompanies his exhibitions, half in jest and half in indignant response to the IACA,

> I hereby swear to the truth of the following statement: I am a full-blood contemporary artist, of the sub-group (or clan) called sculptors. I am not an American Indian, nor have I ever seen or sworn loyalty to India. I am not a Native "American," nor do I feel that "America" has any right to name me or un-name me. I have previously stated that I should be considered mixed blood: that is, I claim to be a male but in fact only one of my parents was male.

Third, and most disturbing, is the fact that the law came into being because of jealousy among Indian artists themselves. Some of these artists formed a group in the Santa Fe area calling themselves the "Native American Artists Association" and persuaded Indian Senator Ben Nighthorse Campbell (R-Colo.) and Polynesian Senator (and chairman of the Senate Select Committee on Indian Affairs) Daniel Inouye (D-Hawaii) to sponsor the bill that led to the IACA. Certainly, such divisiveness within the community of Indian artists itself speaks volumes about the extent to which racial criteria have had and continue to have a destabilizing and deracinating effect on Indian identities, confounding any meaningful discussion of "Indianness," a concept that grows less and less definitive, as perhaps it must, as time and this discussion go on. As historian Limerick has explained, "Set the blood quantum at one-quarter, hold to it as a rigid definition of Indians, let intermarriage proceed as it has for centuries, and eventually Indians will be defined out of existence."[9] Surely, given such a possibility, the criterion of blood quantum must be reconsidered and eventually disavowed as a meaningful marker of Indian identity; yet the fact remains that without a certain quantity of Indian blood, such human beings will in scientific fact cease to belong to the racial group presently called "Indian." Thus the blood quantum argument is a major conundrum that vexes Indian identity at its very core.

A second recent event further enunciates serious discriminatory tendencies within the Indian political community. Writer Ward Churchill and lawyer Glenn Morris, who have both been active members of the Colorado contingent of the American Indian Movement, were "disowned" by the national AIM leadership of Vernon Bellecourt. Churchill had been codirector of the Colorado chapter of AIM since 1980, and Morris had been an activist lawyer for the chapter. Astonishingly, both were dismissed by Bellecourt for "not being Indians" as defined by the IACA, accused of being "wannabe Indians" trying to enhance their respective careers by "posing as Indians." Churchill has published more than one hundred essays on the predicaments of indigenous people in the United States, Canada, and worldwide, and has gained credence as "one of the most outspoken of current Native American activists," as Jace Weaver announced in *Publisher's Weekly*.[10] Ironically, Churchill has consistently opposed the racial bloodline criteria of the IACA, only to find that it is now being applied against him as a political weapon to silence his own "authority." Churchill's most recent volume, *Since Predator Came* (1995), notes of the author that he is an "enrolled associate member of the United Keetoowah Band of Cherokees," an honor he shares with President Bill Clinton. Thus, the criteria by which both Indians and non-Indians are forced into or out of "authenticity" becomes a quagmire of legitimacy and ethics bound to blood quantum, itself a highly controversial and ham-fisted method of establishing identity.

It should further be noted that there is currently a resurgence of indignation among mixed-blood Indians, who challenge the right of full-blooded Indians to dominate the discourse on Indianness. Writers Greg Sarris, Louis Owens, W. S. Penn, and Thomas King, among others, are writing about their mixed-blood heritages with a keen sensibility toward the vitality of hybridization. Returning to the work of Frank Waters, himself "one-tenth" Cheyenne, one can see how mixed-bloods as well as full-bloods can find authentic literary value in their own realizations of Indianness. As Hertha Dawn Wong, a scholar of Indian autobiography, has speculated about her own situation:

> Did my newly discovered part-Indian heritage now make me an "insider," someone who might speak with the authority of belonging? "Of course not," was my first response. Because my ancestry is German, Scotch-Irish, and French as well as Native American, because I do not believe that blood quantum alone determines Indian identity, and because we [her own tribe] do not have a community to which to return, I felt that I could write only as dimly related to, but outside of, the indigenous communities of the United States. But over the years, I have met other displaced mixed-blood people, all of us wrestling with the various labels, the rankings of legitimacy and illegitimacy, imposed on us by others and accepted or resisted by ourselves. . . . As many people have pointed out, so much of twentieth-century Native American experience . . . *is* this experience of multiple marginality.[11]

Clearly, Indian identities continue to be largely determined by racial factors related to the aligned powers of authority, authorship, and authenticity, in the arenas of politics, the fine arts, and literature. Shamed for centuries into concealing their Indian bloodlines from white society and even from their own progeny, some Indians today are faced with an obverse prospect of shame: not being Indian *enough* to claim the rich traditions of Indian history for oneself, to speak of oneself as an Indian, or to claim the spiritual heritage of Indian mythology. Now that many Indians have re-gained the power to "write" their own histories and identities, it seems indeed tragic that some should seek to do so under the same "aegis of a single principle" (genetic racial identification) that has degraded and divided them since contact.

notes

CHAPTER 1

1. Lucy Lippard, *Mixed Blessings* (New York: Pantheon Books, 1990), p. 19.

2. Jean Baudrillard, *Simulations,* trans. Paul Foss, Paul Patton, and Phillip Beitchman (New York: Semiotext(e), 1983), pp. 109–10.

3. C. G. Jung, *The Archetypes and the Collective Unconscious* (Princeton and New York: The Bollingen Series/Princeton University Press, 1969), pp. 3–5.

4. Ibid., p. 38.

5. Roland Barthes, *Mythologies,* trans. Annette Lavers (New York: The Noonday Press, 1972), p. 149.

6. Jung, *The Archetypes,* pp. 5, 7, 30.

7. Barthes, *Mythologies,* pp. 142, 133.

8. Ruth Underhill, *Red Man's Religion* (Chicago and London: University of Chicago Press, 1965), p. 4.

9. Jung, *The Archetypes,* p. 38.

10. Ibid.

11. Ibid., p. 253.

12. See note 16, chapter 2, for a definition and discussion of the term *genocide.*

13. Stephen Trimble, *The People: Indians of the American Southwest* (Santa Fe: School of American Research Press, 1993), p. 58.

CHAPTER 2

1. Herman J. Viola, "Thomas L. McKenney," in Robert M. Kvasnicka and Herman J. Viola, eds., *The Commissioners of Indian Affairs, 1824–1977* (Lincoln and London: University of Nebraska Press, 1979), p. 6.

2. Ronald N. Satz, "Elbert Herring," in Kvasnicka and Viola, *The Commissioners,* p. 12.

3. David E. Stannard, *American Holocaust: Columbus and the Conquest of the New World* (London and New York: Oxford University Press, 1992), p. 123.

4. Satz, "Elbert Herring," p. 13.

5. Robert A. Trennert, "Luke Lea," in Kvasnicka and Viola, *The Commissioners,* p. 52.

6. Robert A. Trennert, "William Medill," in Kvasnicka and Viola, *The Commissioners,* p. 30.

7. Robert A. Trennert, "Orlando Brown," in Kvasnicka and Viola, *The Commissioners,* p. 44.

8. Trennert, "Luke Lea," p. 50.

9. Ibid., p. 54.

10. Gary L. Roberts, "Dennis Nelson Cooley," in Kvasnicka and Viola, *The Commissioners,* p. 102.

11. Carl Waldman, *Encyclopedia of Native American Tribes,* illus. by Molly Braun (New York: Facts on File Publications, 1988), pp. 51–52.

12. Edward E. Hill, "John Q. Smith," in Kvasnicka and Viola, *The Commissioners,* p. 149.

13. Floyd A. O'Neil, "Hiram Price," in Kvasnicka and Viola, *The Commissioners,* p. 175.

14. Michael A. Goldman, "Roland E. Trowbridge," in Kvasnicka and Viola, *The Commissioners,* p. 169.

15. Diane T. Putney, "Robert Grosvenor Valentine," in Kvasnicka and Viola, *The Commissioners,* p. 234.

16. Some modern historians and scholars disallow the use of the term "genocide" in all instances except that of the Holocaust of World War II. Others argue that all internationally accepted definitions of "genocide" should and do include the extermination of the Indian tribes of the Americas and other colonial areas. I have used the word as it was defined by Raphael Lemkin in response to Hitlerian Germany in 1944:

"Generally speaking, genocide does not necessarily mean the immediate destruction of a nation, except when accomplished by mass killings of all members of a nation. It is rather intended to signify a coordinated plan of different actions aimed at the essential foundation of the life of national groups, with the aim of annihilating the groups themselves. The objectives of such a plan would be the disintegration of the political and social institutions of culture, language, national groups, and the destruction of the personal security, liberty, health, dignity, and even the lives of the individuals belonging to such groups. Genocide is directed against individuals, not in their individual capacity, but as members of the national group." See Raphael Lemkin, *Axis Rule in Occupied Europe* (Concord, NH: Carnegie Endowment for International Peace/Rumford Press, 1944), p. 79.

17. George M. Frederickson, *White Supremacy: A Comparative Study in American and South African History* (New York: Oxford University Press, 1981), p. 7.

18. Ronald N. Satz, "Thomas Hartley Crawford," in Kvasnicka and Viola, *The Commissioners,* pp. 25–26.

19. Roberts, "Dennis Nelson Cooley," p. 102.

20. Goldman, "Roland E. Trowbridge," p. 169.

21. Lawrence C. Kelly, "Charles Henry Burke," in Kvasnicka and Viola, *The Commissioners,* p. 259.

22. Lippard, *Mixed Blessings,* p. 209.

23. Underhill, *Red Man's Religion,* p. 211.

24. Lewis Meriam, "A Social Outlook on Indian Missions," in *Facing the Future in Indian Missions* (New York: Council of Women for Home Missions and Missionary Education Movement, 1932), pp. 53–54.

25. Harry Kelsey, "William P. Dole," in Kvasnicka and Viola, *The Commissioners,* p. 96.

26. Gregory C. Thompson, "John D. C. Atkins," in Kvasnicka and Viola, *The Commissioners,* p. 182.

27. Native American Rights Fund, *Newsletter* (Boulder, CO, December 1996).

28. Barthes, *Mythologies,* p. 124.

29. Ibid., p. 155.

30. Trimble, *The People,* p. 450.

31. Underhill, *Red Man's Religion,* p. 235.

32. Oliver La Farge, *As Long As the Grass Shall Grow* (New York and Toronto: Longmans, Green and Co., 1940), p. 77.

33. Baudrillard, *Simulations,* p. 11.

34. Ibid., p. 12.

35. Ibid., p. 109.

36. Ibid., p. 20.

37. Edward Said, *Culture and Imperialism* (New York: Alfred A. Knopf, 1993), p. xix.

38. Raymond William Stedman, *Shadows of the Indian: Stereotypes in American Culture* (Norman: University of Oklahoma Press, 1982), p. 243.

39. W. David Baird, "William A. Jones," in Kvasnicka and Viola, *The Commissioners,* p. 213.

40. Frantz Fanon, *Black Skin, White Masks* (New York: Grove Weidenfeld, 1967), p. 88.

41. Ibid., p. 190.

42. Nathaniel Hawthorne, *The Scarlet Letter,* in Baym et al., eds., *The Norton Anthology of American Literature* (New York and London: W.W. Norton and Company, 1989), p. 1211.

43. Robert F. Berkhofer Jr., *The White Man's Indian: Images of the American Indian from Columbus to the Present* (New York: Alfred A. Knopf, 1978), p. 84.

44. Ibid., p. 27.

CHAPTER 3

1. Robert Meredith and E. Brooks Smith, eds., *Riding with Coronado: From Pedro de Casteñeda's Eyewitness Account of the Exploration of the Southwest* (Boston: Little, Brown and Company, 1964), p. 58.

2. Ibid., p. 38.

3. Alexander Whitaker, *Good Newes from Virginia.* Quoted in Moses Gait Tyler, ed., *A History of American Literature, 1607–1765* (Ithaca, NY: Cornell University Press, 1949), pp. 41–43.

4. Mark Twain, *Roughing It* (Berkeley: University of California Press, 1993 [1872]), p. 98.

5. Stedman, *Shadows of the Indian,* pp. 108–11.

6. Ibid., p. 112.

7. "Artists Who Are Indian." Group show with textual commentary by the artists, who included Rick Bartok (Yurok), Jesse Cooday (Tlingit), Joe Fedderson (Colville-Okanagan), and Susan Stewart (Crow-Blackfeet), among others. The Denver Art Museum, 1994.

8. Georges Sioui, *For an Amerindian Autohistory,* trans. Sheila Fischman (Montreal and Kingston: McGill-Queen's University Press, 1992), p. 64.

9. Berkhofer, *White Man's Indian,* p. 73.

10. Barthes, *Mythologies,* p. 94.

11. Ibid., p. 152.

12. Berkhofer, *White Man's Indian,* p. 29; Baudrillard, *Simulations,* p. 15.

13. Trimble, *The People,* p. 457.

14. Deborah Frazier, "New Agers Damaging Artifacts They Value," *Rocky Mountain News,* 23 June 1994, p. 8A.

15. Rennard Strickland, "Tall Visitor at the Indian Gallery; Or, the Future of Native Ameri-

can Art," in Edwin L. Wade, ed., *The Arts of the North American Indian: Native Tradition in Evolution,* (New York: Hudson Hills Press, 1986), p. 294.

16. "Artists Who Are Indian."

CHAPTER 4

1. Joe Gordon, foreword to *A Selection of Poems by Helen Hunt Jackson and Emily Dickinson* (Colorado Springs, CO: The Hulbert Center Press/The Press at Colorado College, 1990).

2. Valerie Sherer Mathes, foreword to Helen Hunt Jackson, *A Century of Dishonor* (Norman: University of Oklahoma Press, 1995), p. xiii.

3. Ibid., p. xii.

4. Ann Douglas, "Introduction: The Art of Controversy," in Harriet Beecher Stowe, *Uncle Tom's Cabin or, Life Among the Lowly* (New York: Penguin Books, 1981), p. 8.

5. Helen Hunt Jackson, *Ramona* (Boston: Little, Brown & Co., 1884), p. 268.

6. Waldman, *Encyclopedia of North American Tribes,* pp. 135–36.

7. Jackson, *Ramona,* p. 217.

8. Ibid., pp. 45–46.

9. In Stedman, *Shadows of the Indian,* p. 17.

10. Carl Sandburg, "Cool Tombs," in Baym et al., *Norton Anthology of American Literature,* p. 1141.

11. Jackson, *Ramona,* p. 102.

12. Ibid., p. 104.

13. Ibid., pp. 197–98 (emphases added).

14. Ibid., p. 63.

15. Ibid., p. 82.

16. Ibid., p. 354.

17. Ibid., p. 371.

18. Ibid., p. 376.

19. Ibid., p. 87.

20. Ibid., p. 77.

21. Ibid., p. 327.

22. Ibid., p. 42.

CHAPTER 5

1. Win Blevins, "A Tribute to *The Man Who Killed the Deer,*" in Vine Deloria Jr., ed., *Frank Waters: Man and Mystic,* (Athens, OH: Ohio University Press/Swallow Press, 1993), p. 151.

2. Oliver La Farge, *Laughing Boy* (New York: Houghton Mifflin, 1957 [1929]), p. x.

3. D'Arcy McNickle, *Indian Man: A Life of Oliver La Farge* (Bloomington and London: Indiana University Press, 1971), p. 50.

4. La Farge, *Laughing Boy,* p. xi.

5. Ibid., book jacket.

6. McNickle, *Indian Man,* p. 54.

7. La Farge, *Laughing Boy,* p. vii.

8. Walt Whitman, "Passage to India," in Baym et al., *The Norton Anthology of American Literature*, pp. 2062–68.

9. T. C. McLuhan, *Dream Tracks: The Railroad and the American Indian 1890–1930* (New York: Harry N. Abrams, 1985), p. 27.

10. Ibid.

11. Gary Snyder, *Turtle Island* (New York: New Directions, 1969), p. 3.

12. La Farge, *Laughing Boy,* p. 150.

13. Ibid., p. 128.

14. Ibid., p. 115.

15. Ibid., pp. 72–73.

16. Washington Matthews, trans. and coll., *Navaho Legends* (Boston and New York: Houghton, Mifflin and Co., 1897; Millwood, NY: Kraus Reprint Co., 1976), p. 35. The standard Navajo form of this name is Naayéé' Neizghání, with the meaning "monster slayer"; see Leland C. Wyman, "Navajo Ceremonial System," in William C. Sturtevant, ed., *Handbook of North American Indians,* vol. 10: *Southwest,* ed. Alfonso Ortiz (Washington, DC: Smithsonian Institution Press, 1983), p. 539.

17. La Farge, *Laughing Boy,* p. 50.

18. Trimble, *The People,* p. 146.

19. Underhill, *Red Man's Religion,* pp. 98–99.

20. La Farge, *Laughing Boy,* p. 78.

21. Ibid., p. 258.

22. Ibid., p. 261.

23. Ibid., p. 233.

24. Matthews, *Navaho Legends,* p. 275.

25. Trimble, *The People,* p. 127.

26. La Farge, *Laughing Boy,* p. 32.

27. Ibid., p. 34.

28. Underhill, *Red Man's Religion,* p. 98.

29. La Farge, *Laughing Boy,* p. 74.

30. Ibid., p. 161.

31. Ibid., pp. 136, 139.

32. Ibid., p. 284.

33. Jung, *The Archetypes,* p. 32.

34. La Farge, *Laughing Boy,* p. 302.

35. Beverly Slapin and Doris Seale, eds., *Through Indian Eyes: The Native Experience in Books for Children* (Philadelphia: New Society Publishers, 1992), p. 16.

36. Stedman, *Shadows of the Indian,* p. 60.

37. La Farge, *Laughing Boy,* p. 171.

38. See Kenneth R. Philp, *John Collier's Crusade for Reform, 1920–1954* (Tucson: University of Arizona Press, 1977) for a close analysis of the progressive turn in the BIA under Collier. Despite the fact that intellectuals such as La Farge and Collier tried to impose too many of their own socializing visions on various Indian tribes, they also helped end the devastating effects of

the Allotment Act and in general acted in what they believed were the best interests of Indians. "[Collier] awakened in the souls of many natives, not only pride in being Indian, but hope for the future as Indians" (p. 213).

39. McNickle, *Indian Man,* p. 61.

CHAPTER 6

1. McLuhan, *Dream Tracks,* p. 18.
2. D. Duane Cummins, *William Robinson Leigh: Western Artist* (Norman: University of Oklahoma Press, 1980), p. 6.
3. Ibid., p. 87.
4. McLuhan, *Dream Tracks,* p. 19.
5. Cummins, *William Robinson Leigh,* p. xvi.
6. Matthews, *Navaho Legends,* p. 45.
7. Cummins, *William Robinson Leigh,* pp. 3–4.
8. Matthews, *Navaho Legends,* p. 38.
9. June DuBois, *W. R. Leigh: The Definitive Illustrated Biography* (Kansas City: Lowell Press, 1977), p. 96.
10. Quoted in DuBois, *W. R. Leigh,* pp. 103–4.
11. P. David Seaman, ed., *Born a Chief: The Nineteenth Century Hopi Boyhood of Edmund Nequatewa* (Tucson: University of Arizona Press, 1993), p. 76.
12. Barthes, *Mythologies,* p. 95.
13. John Ford, dir., *The Searchers,* videocassette, VHS, color, 119 min. (Burbank, CA: Werner Home Video, 1984 [1956]).
14. David L. Witt, *The Taos Artists* (Colorado Springs, CO: Ewell Fine Arts Publications, 1992), p. 4.
15. Sherry Clayton Taggett and Ted Schwarz, *Paintbrushes and Pistols: How the Taos Artists Sold the West* (Santa Fe: John Muir Publications, 1990), p. 157.
16. McLuhan, *Dream Tracks,* p. 28.
17. Taggett and Schwarz, *Paintbrushes and Pistols,* p. 77.
18. Trimble, *The People,* p. 78.
19. Patricia Broder, *Taos: A Painter's Dream* (Boston: New York Graphics Society/Little, Brown & Co., 1980), p. 108.
20. Taggett and Schwarz, *Paintbrushes and Pistols,* p. 108.
21. Ibid., p. 113.
22. Baird, "William A. Jones," p. 214.
23. Taggett and Schwarz, *Paintbrushes and Pistols,* p. 120.
24. Ibid., p. 178.
25. Broder, *Taos,* p. 216.
26. Ibid., p. 225.
27. Ibid., p. 227.
28. Ibid., p. 179.
29. McLuhan, *Dream Tracks,* p. 33.
30. Taggett and Schwarz, *Paintbrushes and Pistols,* pp. 190–94.

31. McLuhan, *Dream Tracks,* p. 31.

32. Taggett and Schwarz, *Paintbrushes and Pistols,* p. 169.

CHAPTER 7

1. Kenneth R. Philp, "John Collier," in Kvasnicka and Viola, *The Commissioners,* p. 274.

2. John Collier, *On the Gleaming Way* (Denver: Sage Books, 1962 [1949]), p. 38.

3. Ibid., pp. 90–97.

4. Ibid., p. 115.

5. Ibid., p. 128.

6. Philp, *John Collier's Crusade,* p. 111.

7. David Jongeward, "Frank Waters," in Vine Deloria Jr., *Frank Waters,* p. 25.

8. Charles Hathaway and Barbara Waters, "Bijou Street Beginnings," in Vine Deloria Jr., *Frank Waters,* p. 43.

9. Frank Waters, *The Book of the Hopi* (New York: Viking Penguin, 1977 [1963]), p. ix.

10. Ibid., p. xiv.

11. Ibid., p. 4.

12. Charles L. Adams, ed., *Frank Waters: A Retrospective Anthology* (Athens, OH: Swallow Press/Ohio University Press, 1985), p. 113.

13. Waters, *Book of the Hopi,* p. 19.

14. Ibid., pp. 10–11.

15. Ibid., pp. 26–27.

16. In Donald Cordry, *Mexican Masks* (Austin: University of Texas Press, 1980), p. 142.

17. Waters, *Book of the Hopi,* pp. 134–35.

18. Ibid., p. 125.

19. Ibid., p. 144.

20. Underhill, *Red Man's Religion,* p. 42.

21. Quay Grigg, "Masking the Self," in Vine Deloria Jr., *Frank Waters,* p. 163.

22. Blevins, "A Tribute," p. 152.

23. Frank Waters, *The Man Who Killed the Deer* (Athens, OH: Swallow Press/Ohio University Press, 1994 [1942]), p. 26.

24. Ibid., pp. 27, 29.

25. Ibid., p. 31.

26. Ibid., p. 153.

27. Barthes, *Mythologies,* p. 135.

28. Waters, *The Man Who Killed the Deer,* p. 188.

29. Thomas H. Johnson, ed., *The Complete Poems of Emily Dickinson* (Boston: Little, Brown and Company, 1960), p. 100.

30. Waters, *The Man Who Killed the Deer,* p. 14.

31. Ibid., p. 135.

32. Ibid., p. 161.

33. Quay Grigg, "The Sounds of Silence in Frank Waters's Novels," in Charles Adams, ed., *Studies in Frank Waters—VII: An Appreciation* (Las Vegas, NV: The Frank Waters Society, 1986), p. 39.

34. Ibid., p. 34.

35. Baudrillard, *Simulations,* pp. 11–12.

36. Father Peter J. Powell, "The Presence of the Sacred," in Vine Deloria Jr., *Frank Waters,* p. 182.

37. Paul de Man, "Semiology and Rhetoric," in Charles Kaplan, ed., *Criticism: The Major Statements* (New York: St. Martin's Press, 1986), p. 615.

38. Waters, *The Man Who Killed the Deer,* pp. 106, 190.

39. Ibid., p. 207.

40. Stedman, *Shadows of the Indian,* p. 251.

41. Vine Deloria Jr., "Frank Waters: Prophet and Explorer," in *Frank Waters,* p. 167.

42. Frank Waters, *Pumpkin Seed Point: Being Within the Hopi* (Athens, OH: Swallow Press/ Ohio University Press, 1981 [1969]), pp. 2, 4.

43. Waldman, *Encylopedia of North American Tribes,* p. 98.

44. See also Underhill, *Red Man's Religion,* p. 155.

45. Waters, *Pumpkin Seed Point,* p. 14.

46. Ibid., p. 5.

47. Ibid.

48. Collier, *On the Gleaming Way,* p. 45.

49. Grigg, "Masking the Self," p. 164.

50. Trimble, *The People,* p. 45.

51. Mircea Eliade, *Shamanism: Archaic Techniques of Ecstasy* (New York: The Bollingen Foundation, 1964), p. 78.

52. Waters, *Pumpkin Seed Point,* p. 13.

53. Ibid., p. 20.

54. Ibid., p. 120.

55. Barthes, *Mythologies,* p. 142.

56. Waters, *Pumpkin Seed Point,* p. 122.

57. Some scholars contend that Hitlerian Germany purposefully adopted United States Indian policy in its programs of "ethnic cleansing" and lebensraum. There is also some evidence that South Africa's white ruling class used this same American model for its apartheid policies.

58. Waters, *Pumpkin Seed Point,* p. 124.

59. Ibid., p. 125.

CHAPTER 8

1. Said, *Culture and Imperialism,* p. 195.

2. Fanon, *Black Skin, White Masks,* p. 204.

3. Lippard, *Mixed Blessings,* p. 20.

4. Strickland, "Tall Visitor at the Indian Gallery," p. 294.

5. Peggy Samuels and Harold Samuels, *Contemporary Western Artists* (New York: Bonanza Books, 1982), p. 12.

6. Ibid., p. 148.

7. Ibid., p. 178.

8. Ibid., p. 176 (emphasis added).

9. Ibid., p. 5 (emphasis added).

10. Baudrillard, *Simulations,* pp. 12–13.

11. Philp, "John Collier," p. 276.

12. Jamake Highwater, "Controversy in Native American Art," in Wade, *Arts of the North American Indian,* p. 223. I quote Highwater with the full awareness of his dubious standing as an ethnic Native American, a controversy that has surrounded him since Hank Adams's extensive research into Highwater's work *Primal Mind,* a work that purports to be seminally Indian, as Highwater maintained of himself. Adams, in the late 1980s, successfully exposed Highwater as an Anglo writer who in his twenties was named Jay Marks and was possibly born a Greek named Gregory Marcoupolos. Highwater is rumored to have died in 1994, leaving a legacy of uncertainty as to his real identity. His scholarship regarding Native art, however, remains solid and unimpeached.

13. Gerhard Hoffman, "Frames of Reference: Native American Art in the Context of Modern and Postmodern Art," in Wade, *Arts of the North American Indian,* p. 263.

14. Highwater, "Controversy in Native American Art," p. 224.

15. Ibid.

16. See Joan Frederick, *T. C. Cannon: He Stood in the Sun* (Flagstaff, AZ: Northland Publishing, 1995), for an intimate history of the brief, ingenious life of Cannon.

17. See Hoffman, "Frames of Reference," for a history of emerging, "new wave" Indian artists of the 1950s and later.

18. See Ian M. Thom, *Robert Davidson: Eagle of the Dawn* (Seattle: University of Washington Press, 1993) for a lavish and well-documented history of Davidson's unique work.

19. Strickland, "Tall Visitor at the Indian Gallery," p. 386.

20. Hoffman, "Frames of Reference," p. 257.

21. Ibid., p. 287.

22. Highwater, "Controversy in Native American Art," p. 228.

23. Hoffman, "Frames of Reference," p. 263.

24. Lippard, *Mixed Blessings,* p. 27.

25. Jung, *The Archetypes,* p. 7.

26. Waters, *Book of the Hopi,* p. 167.

27. William S. Burroughs and Brion Gysin, *The Third Mind* (New York: Viking Press, 1978), p. 31.

28. Lippard, *Mixed Blessings,* p. 214.

29. Hoffman, "Frames of Reference," p. 278.

30. Peter T. Furst and Jill L. Furst, *North American Indian Art* (New York: Rizzoli International Publications, 1982), p. 169. See also Joyce M. Szabo, *Howling Wolf and the History of Ledger Art* (Albuquerque: University of New Mexico Press, 1994) and Richard W. West Jr. et al., *Robes of Splendor: Native North American Painted Buffalo Hides,* English language edition (New York: The New Press, 1993) for in-depth commentary on traditional Plains Indian hide paintings and their resurgence as "art" during the 1870s, when several Plains leaders were imprisoned at Fort Marion, Florida, and took up illustrating their histories, both modern and ancient, on ledger books provided to them by their military captors.

31. Highwater, "Controversy in Native American Art," p. 237.

32. Jung, *The Archetypes,* p. 5.

CHAPTER 9

1. Vera Laski, "The Text of the Rain God Drama," in Jerome Rothenberg, ed., *Shaking the Pumpkin* (New York: Doubleday, 1972 [Albuquerque: University of New Mexico Press, 1991]), p. 2; emphasis in original.

2. Arnold Krupat, ed., "Introduction," *Native American Autobiography: An Anthology* (Madison: University of Wisconsin Press, 1994), p. 3.

3. Hertha D. Wong, *Sending My Heart Back Across the Years: Tradition and Innovation in Native American Autobiography* (Oxford and New York: Oxford University Press, 1992), p. 14; and H. David Brumble III, *American Indian Autobiography* (Berkeley and Los Angeles: University of California Press, 1988).

4. Brumble, *American Indian Autobiography,* p. 11.

5. "Letters of Catharine Brown," December 1818, in Krupat, *Native American Autobiography,* p. 118.

6. A. LaVonne Brown Ruoff, "Western American Indian Writers, 1854–1960," in Thomas J. Lyon, ed., *A Literary History of the American West,* Sponsored by the Western Literary Association (Ft. Worth: Texas Christian University Press, 1987), p. 1041.

7. See Krupat, "Introduction," for a fairly inclusive selection of Native autobiographies. See also Brian Swann and Arnold Krupat, eds., *I Tell You Now: Autobiographical Essays by Native American Writers* (Lincoln: University of Nebraska Press, 1987).

8. Ruoff, "Western American Indian Writers," p. 1038.

9. Ibid., p. 1048.

10. Louis Owens, *Other Destinies: Understanding the American Indian Novel* (Norman and London: University of Oklahoma Press, 1992), p. 40.

11. Paula Gunn Allen, *Voice of the Turtle: American Indian Literature 1900–1970* (New York: Ballantine Books, 1994).

12. Garrick Baily, "John Joseph Mathews," in Margot Liberty, ed., *American Indian Intellectuals: 1976,* Proceedings of the American Ethnological Society (St. Paul, MN: West, 1978), p. 210.

13. Robert Allen Warrior, *Tribal Secrets: Recovering American Indian Intellectual Traditions* (Minneapolis: University of Minnesota Press, 1995), p. 23.

14. Ibid., p. 54.

15. Owens, *Other Destinies,* p. 60.

16. Ibid., p. 18.

17. Ruoff, "Western American Indian Writers," p. 1051.

18. Owens, *Other Destinies,* p. 79. It should be noted here that an unpublished version of *The Surrounded* offers a less fatalistic version of the same story, which is taken by Owens to be the better and more characteristic version in his essay on McNickle.

19. Ibid., p. 95.

20. Kenneth Lincoln, *Native American Renaissance* (Berkeley and Los Angeles: University of California Press, 1983), p. 157.

21. Leslie Marmon Silko, *Ceremony* (New York: Viking Penguin, 1977), p. 53.

22. Ibid., p. 249.

23. Linda Hogan, *Mean Spirit* (New York: Atheneum/Macmillan, 1990), p. 13.

24. Ibid., p. 12.

25. Ibid., p. 10.

26. Ibid., p. 31.

27. Ibid., 337.

28. Ibid., p. 273.

29. Ibid., p. 174.

30. Ibid., pp. 254–55.

31. Ibid., p. 280.

32. Ibid., p. 274.

33. Ibid., p. 238.

34. Ibid., p. 337.

35. Ibid., p. 270.

36. Vine Deloria Jr., *Red Earth, White Lies* (New York: Scribner, 1995), p. 27.

37. Underhill, *Red Man's Religion*, p. 65.

38. Sherman Alexie, *Reservation Blues* (New York: Atlantic Monthly Press, 1995), pp. 9–10.

39. Ibid., p. 174.

40. Ibid., p. 10.

41. Ibid., p. 36.

42. Ibid., p. 179.

43. Ibid., pp. 130–31.

44. Ibid., p. 148.

45. Ibid., pp. 140–41.

46. Ibid., p. 184.

47. Ibid., p. 206.

48. Ibid., p. 302.

49. Ibid., p. 158.

50. Ibid., p. 168.

51. Sherman Alexie, *First Indian on the Moon* (Brooklyn, NY: Hanging Loose Press, 1993), p. 9.

52. Alexie, *Reservation Blues*, pp. 151, 183.

53. Jung, *The Archetypes*, p. 38.

54. Alexie, *First Indian on the Moon*, p. 36.

55. Alexie, *Reservation Blues*, p. 36.

56. Adrian C. Louis, "Foreword," in Sherman Alexie, *Old Shirts & New Skins* (Los Angeles: American Indian Studies Center, University of California, 1993), p. viii.

57. Simon J. Ortiz, *After and Before the Lightning* (Tucson and London: University of Arizona Press, 1994), p. xv.

58. Ibid., pp. 70–71.

59. Ibid., p. 40.

60. Ibid., p. 75.

61. Ibid., pp. 100–101.

62. Ibid., p. 101.

63. Ibid., p. 39.

64. Ibid., p. 86.

65. From "Foolish Believers," ibid., pp. 25–26.

66. Andrew Wiget, *Simon Ortiz,* Western Writers Series, no. 74 (Boise, ID: Boise State University, 1986), p. 44.

67. Ortiz, *After and Before the Lightning,* p. 4.

68. Ibid., p. 103.

69. Paula Gunn Allen, "Western American Indian Poetry, 1968–1983," in Thomas J. Lyon, ed., *A Literary History of the American West,* Sponsored by the Western Literary Association (Ft. Worth: Texas Christian University Press, 1987), p. 1075.

70. Wong, *Sending My Heart Back,* p. 16.

71. Ortiz, *After and Before the Lightning,* p. xv.

72. Ibid., pp. 88–90.

73. Original statistics available from U.S. Department of Health and Human Services, *Chart Series Book* (Washington, DC: Public Health Service, 1988 [HE20.9409.988]).

74. Ortiz, *After and Before the Lightning,* p. 12.

75. Ibid., pp. 90–91.

CHAPTER 10

1. Phillip J. Deloria, "The Twentieth Century and Beyond," in Betty Ballantine and Ian Ballantine, eds., *The Native Americans: An Illustrated History* (Atlanta: Turner Publishing, 1993), p. 433.

2. "300,000 Indians Sue Federal Government for Mismanaging Their Money," *Native American Rights Fund Legal Review* 21(2)(summer/fall 1996):1.

3. Philip A. May, "The Epidemiology of Alcohol Abuse Among Indians: The Mythical and Real Properties," *American Indian Culture and Research Journal* 18(2)(1994):122.

4. Thomas W. Sweeney, "Fact Sheet," 2 August 1995 (Washington, DC: U.S. Department of the Interior/Bureau of Indian Affairs).

5. "Tribal Leaders Rip Budget Cuts," *Rocky Mountain News,* 24 August 1995, p. 10A.

6. "Indians Blast Cuts in Funding," *Rocky Mountain News,* 3 August 1995, p. 40A.

7. Deloria, "Twentieth Century and Beyond," pp. 445–46.

8. Fergus M. Bordewich, *Killing the White Man's Indian: Reinventing Native Americans at the End of the Twentieth Century* (New York: Doubleday, 1996), p. 338.

9. Patricia Nelson Limerick, *The Legacy of Conquest: The Unbroken Past of the American West* (New York: W.W. Norton and Co., 1987), p. 338.

10. Jace Weaver, book jacket blurb, on Ward Churchill, *Indians Are Us?* (Monroe, ME: Common Courage Press, 1994).

11. Wong, *Sending My Heart Back,* p. iii.

bibliography

Adams, Charles L., ed. *Frank Waters: A Retrospective Anthology*. Athens, OH: Swallow Press/ Ohio University Press, 1985.

——. ed. *Studies in Frank Waters—VII: An Appreciation*. Las Vegas, NV: The Frank Waters Society, 1986.

Alexie, Sherman. *First Indian on the Moon*. Brooklyn, NY: Hanging Loose Press, 1993.

——. *Old Shirts & New Skins*. Los Angeles: American Indian Studies Center/University of California, 1993.

——. *Reservation Blues*. New York: The Atlantic Monthly Press, 1995.

Allen, Paula Gunn. *Voice of the Turtle: American Indian Literature, 1900–1970*. New York: Ballantine Books, 1994.

——. "Western American Indian Poetry, 1968–1983." In Thomas J. Lyon, ed., *A Literary History of the American West*, pp. 1067–75. Sponsored by the Western Literary Association. Ft. Worth: Texas Christian University Press, 1987.

Apess, William. *The Experiences of Five Christian Indians of the Pequot Tribe*. Boston: James B. Dow, 1833.

"Artists Who Are Indian." Group show with textual commentary by the artists, who included Rick Bartok (Yurok), Jesse Cooday (Tlingit), Joe Fedderson (Colville-Okanagan), and Susan Stewart (Crow-Blackfeet). The Denver Art Museum, 1994.

Baily, Garrick. "John Joseph Mathews." In Margot Liberty, ed., *American Indian Intellectuals: 1976*. Proceedings of the American Ethnological Society. St. Paul, MN: West, 1978.

Baird, W. David. "William A. Jones." In Kvasnicka and Viola, *The Commissioners*, 1979, pp. 211–20.

Barthes, Roland. *Mythologies*. Trans. Annette Lavers. New York: Noonday Press, 1972.

Baudrillard, Jean. *Simulations*. Trans. Paul Foss, Paul Patton, and Phillip Beitchman. New York: Semiotext(e), 1983.

Baym, Nina, Ronald Gottesman, Laurence B. Holland, David Kalstone, Francis Murphy, Hershel Parker, William H. Pritchard, and Patricia B. Wallace, eds. *The Norton Anthology of American Literature*. 3rd ed. Vol. 2. New York and London: W. W. Norton and Co., 1989.

Berkhofer, Robert F., Jr. *The White Man's Indian: Images of the American Indian from Columbus to the Present*. New York: Alfred A. Knopf, 1978.

Bigfeather, Joanna Osburn. *Portfolio III: Ten Contemporary Indian Artists*. San Francisco and Seattle: American Indian Contemporary Artists/Marquand Books, 1991.

Blevins, Win. "A Tribute to *The Man Who Killed the Deer*." In Vine Deloria Jr., *Frank Waters,* 1993, pp. 149–55.

Bordewich, Fergus M. *Killing the White Man's Indian: Reinventing Native Americans at the End of the Twentieth Century.* New York: Doubleday, 1996.

Broder, Patricia. *Taos: A Painter's Dream.* Boston: New York Graphics Society/Little, Brown & Co., 1980.

Brumble, H. David III. *American Indian Autobiography.* Berkeley and Los Angeles: University of California Press, 1988.

Burroughs, William S., and Brion Gysin. *The Third Mind.* New York: Viking Press, 1978.

Churchill, Ward. *Indians Are Us?* Monroe, ME: Common Courage Press, 1994.

Collier, John. *On the Gleaming Way.* Denver: Sage Books, 1962 [1949].

Cordry, Donald. *Mexican Masks.* Austin: University of Texas Press, 1980.

Cummins, D. Duane. *William Robinson Leigh: Western Artist.* Norman: University of Oklahoma Press, 1980.

Deloria, Phillip J. "The Twentieth Century and Beyond," in Betty Ballantine and Ian Ballantine, eds., *The Native Americans: An Illustrated History.* Atlanta: Turner Publishing, 1993.

Deloria, Vine, Jr. "Frank Waters: Prophet and Explorer." In Vine Deloria Jr., *Frank Waters,* 1993, pp. 166–73.

——. *Red Earth, White Lies.* New York: Scribner, 1995.

Deloria, Vine, Jr., ed. *Frank Waters: Man and Mystic.* Athens, OH: Ohio University Press/Swallow Press, 1993.

De Man, Paul. "Semiology and Rhetoric." In Charles Kaplan, *Criticism,* pp. 606–22.

Douglas, Ann. "Introduction: The Art of Controversy." In Harriet Beecher Stowe, *Uncle Tom's Cabin or, Life Among the Lowly.* New York: Penguin Books, 1981.

DuBois, June. *W. R. Leigh: The Definitive Illustrated Biography.* Kansas City: Lowell Press, 1977.

Eastman, Charles. *From the Deep Woods to Civilization: Chapters in the Autobiography of an Indian.* Boston: Little, Brown and Co., 1916.

Eliade, Mircea. *Shamanism: Archaic Techniques of Ecstasy.* New York: Bollingen Foundation, 1964.

Fanon, Frantz. *Black Skin, White Masks.* New York: Grove Weidenfeld, 1967.

Ford, John, dir. *The Searchers.* Videocassette. VHS, color, 119 min. Burbank, CA: Warner Home Video, 1984 [1956].

Fonseca, Henry. *Portfolio III: Ten Contemporary Indian Artists.* San Francisco and Seattle: American Indian Contemporary Artists/Marquand Books, 1991.

Frazier, Deborah. "New Agers Damaging Artifacts They Value." *Rocky Mountain News,* 23 June 1994, p. 8A.

Frederick, Joan. *T. C. Cannon: He Stood in the Sun.* Flagstaff, AZ: Northland Publishing, 1995.

Frederickson, George M. *White Supremacy: A Comparative Study in American and South African History .* Cambridge: Oxford University Press, 1981.

Furst, Peter T., and Jill L. Furst. *North American Indian Art.* New York: Rizzoli International Publications, 1982.

Goodman, Michael A. "Roland E. Trowbridge." In Kvasnicka and Viola, *The Commissioners,* 1979, pp. 167–72.

Gordon, Joe. "Foreword." In *A Selection of Poems by Helen Hunt Jackson and Emily Dickinson.* Colorado Springs, CO: Hulbert Center Press/The Press at Colorado College, 1990.

Grigg, Quay. "Masking the Self." In Vine Deloria Jr., *Frank Waters,* 1993, pp. 156–65.

——. "The Sounds of Silence in Frank Waters's Novels." In Charles Adams, *Studies in Frank Waters,* pp. 27–43.

Hathaway Charles, and Barbara Waters. "Bijou Street Beginnings." In Vine Deloria Jr., *Frank Waters,* 1993, pp. 39–52.

Hawthorne, Nathaniel. *The Scarlet Letter.* In Baym et al., *Norton Anthology,* 1989 [1850], pp. 1162–1301.

Highwater, Jamake. "Controversy in Native American Art." In Wade, *Arts of the North American Indian,* 1986, pp. 223–42.

——. *The Primal Mind: Vision and Reality in Indian America.* New York: Harper and Row, 1981.

Hill, Edward E. "John Q. Smith." In Kvasnicka and Viola, *The Commissioners,* 1979, pp. 149–54.

Hoffman, Gerhard. "Frames of Reference: Native American Art in the Context of Modern and Postmodern Art." In Wade, *Arts of the North American Indian,* 1986, pp. 257–82.

Hogan, Linda. *Mean Spirit.* New York: Atheneum/Macmillan, 1990.

Hopkins, Sarah Winnemucca. *Life Among the Paiutes: Their Wrongs and Claims.* Reno: University of Nevada Press, 1994 [1883].

"Indians Blast Cuts in Funding." *Rocky Mountain News,* 3 August 1995, p. 40A.

Jackson, Helen Hunt. *A Century of Dishonor: A Sketch of the United States Government's Dealings with Some of the Indian Tribes.* Norman: University of Oklahoma, 1995 [1885].

——. *Ramona.* Boston: Little, Brown and Co., 1884.

Johnson, Thomas H., ed. *The Complete Poems of Emily Dickinson .* Boston: Little, Brown and Co., 1960.

Jongeward, David. "Frank Waters." In Vine Deloria Jr., *Frank Waters,* 1993, pp. 15–32.

Jung, C. G. *The Archetypes and the Collective Unconscious.* Princeton and New York: The Bollingen Series/Princeton University Press, 1969.

Kaplan, Charles, ed. *Criticism: The Major Statements.* New York: St. Martin's Press, 1986.

Kelly, Lawrence C. "Charles Henry Burke." In Kvasnicka and Viola, *The Commissioners,* 1979, pp. 251–62.

Kelsey, Harry. "William P. Dole." In Kvasnicka and Viola, *The Commissioners,* 1979, pp. 89–98.

Krupat, Arnold, ed. "Introduction." In *Native American Autobiography: An Anthology.* Madison: University of Wisconsin Press, 1994.

Kvasnicka, Robert M., and Herman J. Viola, eds. *The Commissioners of Indian Affairs, 1824–1977.* Lincoln and London: University of Nebraska Press, 1979.

La Farge, Oliver. *As Long as the Grass Shall Grow.* New York and Toronto: Longman's, Green & Co., 1940.

——. *Laughing Boy.* New York: Houghton Mifflin, 1957 [1929].

LaFlesche, Francis. *The Middle Five: Indian Schoolboys of the Omaha Tribe.* Madison: University of Wisconsin Press, 1963 [1900].

Laski, Vera. "The Text of the Rain God Drama." In Jerome Rothenberg, ed., *Shaking the Pumpkin.* New York: Doubleday, 1972 [Albuquerque: University of New Mexico Press, 1991].

Lemkin, Raphael. *Axis Rule in Occupied Europe.* Concord, NH: Carnegie Endowment for International Peace/Rumford Press, 1944.

Limerick, Patricia Nelson. *The Legacy of Conquest: The Unbroken Past of the American West.* New York: W. W. Norton and Co., 1987.

Lincoln, Kenneth. *Native American Renaissance.* Berkeley: University of California Press, 1983.

Lippard, Lucy. *Mixed Blessings.* New York: Pantheon Books, 1990.

Louis, Adrian C. "Foreword." In Sherman Alexie, *Old Shirts & New Skins.* Los Angeles: American Indian Studies Center, University of California Press, 1993.

Lyon, Thomas J., ed. *A Literary History of the American West.* Sponsored by the Western Literary Association. Ft. Worth: Texas Christian University Press, 1987.

Mathes, Valerie Sherer. "Foreword." In Helen Hunt Jackson, *A Century of Dishonor.* Norman: University of Oklahoma Press, 1995 [1880].

Mathews, John Joseph. *Sundown.* Norman: University of Oklahoma Press, 1988 [1934].

——. *Talking to the Moon: Wildlife Adventures on the Prairies and Plains of Osage Country.* Norman: University of Oklahoma Press, 1945.

——. *Wah'Kon-Tah: The Osage and the White Man's Road.* Norman: University of Oklahoma Press, 1932.

Matthews, Washington, trans. and coll. *Navaho Legends.* Millwood, NY: Kraus Reprint Co., 1976 [1897].

May, Philip A. "The Epidemiology of Alcohol Abuse Among Indians: The Mythical and Real Properties." *American Indian Culture and Research Journal* 18(2)(1994).

McLuhan, T. C. *Dream Tracks: The Railroad and the American Indian 1890–1930.* New York: Harry N. Abrams, 1985.

McNickle, D'Arcy. *Indian Man: A Life of Oliver La Farge.* Bloomington and London: Indiana University Press, 1971.

——. *The Surrounded.* Albuquerque: University of New Mexico Press, 1978 [1936].

——. *Wind from an Enemy Sky.* Albuquerque: University of New Mexico Press, 1988 [1979].

Meredith, Robert, and E. Brooks Smith, eds. *Riding with Coronado: From Pedro de Casteñeda's Eyewitness Account of the Exploration of the Southwest.* Boston: Little, Brown and Co., 1964.

Meriam, Lewis. "A Social Outlook on Indian Missions." In *Facing the Future in Indian Missions,* pp. 3–144. New York: Council of Women for Home Missions and Missionary Education Movement, 1932.

Momaday, N. Scott. *House Made of Dawn.* New York: Harper and Row, 1968.

——. *The Names: A Memoir.* New York: Harper and Row, 1976.

——. *The Way to Rainy Mountain.* Albuquerque: University of New Mexico Press, 1969.

Mourning Dove (Hum-Ishu-Ma). *Cogewea: The Half-Blood.* Lincoln and London: University of Nebraska Press, 1981.

O'Neil, Floyd A. "Hiram Price." In Kvasnicka and Viola, *The Commissioners,* 1979, pp. 173–80.

Ortiz, Simon. *After and Before the Lightning.* Tucson and London: University of Arizona Press, 1994.

Oskison, John Milton. *Brothers Three.* New York: Macmillan, 1935.

Owens, Louis. *Other Destinies: Understanding the American Indian Novel.* Norman: University of Oklahoma Press, 1992.

Philp, Kenneth R. "John Collier." In Kvasnicka and Viola, *The Commissioners,* 1979, pp. 273–82.

———. *John Collier's Crusade for Reform, 1920–1954.* Tucson: University of Arizona Press, 1977.

Pokagon, Somon. *O-gi-Maw-Kwe Mit-i-gwa-ki (Queen of the Woods).* Berrien Springs, MI: Hardscrabble Books, 1972 [1899].

Powell, Father Peter J. "The Presence of the Sacred." In Vine Deloria Jr., *Frank Waters,* 1993, pp. 174–82.

Putney, Diane T. "Robert Grosvenor Valentine." In Kvasnicka and Viola, *The Commissioners,* 1979, pp. 233–42.

Ridge, John Rollin. *The Life and Adventures of Joaquin Murietta, the Celebrated California Bandit.* Norman: University of Oklahoma Press, 1977 [1854].

Roberts, Gary L. "Dennis Nelson Cooley." In Kvasnicka and Viola, *The Commissioners,* 1979, pp. 99–108.

Ruoff, A LaVonne Brown. "Western American Indian Writers, 1854–1960." In Thomas J. Lyon, ed., *A Literary History of the American West,* pp. 1038–78. Sponsored by The Western Literary Association. Ft. Worth: Texas Christian University Press, 1987.

Said, Edward. *Culture and Imperialism.* New York: Alfred A. Knopf, 1993.

Samuels, Peggy, and Harold Samuels. *Contemporary Western Artists.* New York: Bonanza Books, 1982.

Satz, Ronald N. "Elbert Herring." In Kvasnicka and Viola, *The Commissioners,* 1979, pp. 13–16.

———. "Thomas Hartley Crawford." In Kvasnicka and Viola, *The Commissioners,* 1979, pp. 23–28.

Schimmel, Julie, and Robert R. White. *Bert Geer Phillips and the Taos Art Colony.* Albuquerque: University of New Mexico Press, 1994.

Seaman, P. David, ed. *Born a Chief: The Nineteenth Century Hopi Boyhood of Edmund Nequatewa.* Tucson: University of Arizona Press, 1993.

Silko, Leslie Marmon. *Ceremony.* New York: Viking Penguin, 1977.

———. *Storyteller.* New York: Seaver Books, 1981.

Sioui, Georges E. *For an Amerindian Autohistory.* Trans. by Sheila Fischman. Montreal and Kingston: McGill-Queen's University Press, 1992.

Slapin, Beverly, and Doris Seale, eds. *Through Indian Eyes: The Native Experience in Books for Children.* Philadelphia: New Society Publishers, 1992.

Snyder, Gary. *Turtle Island.* New York: New Directions, 1969.

Stannard, David E. *American Holocaust: Columbus and the Conquest of the New World.* London and New York: Oxford University Press, 1992.

Stedman, Raymond William. *Shadows of the Indian: Stereotypes in American Culture.* Norman: University of Oklahoma Press, 1982.

Strickland, Rennard. "Tall Visitor at the Indian Gallery; or, the Future of Native American Art." In Wade, *Arts of the North American Indian,* 1986, pp. 283–306.

Sturtevant, William C., ed. *Handbook of North American Indians.* Vol. 10: *Southwest,* ed. Alfonso Ortiz. Washington, DC: Smithsonian Institution Press, 1983.

Swann, Brian, and Arnold Krupat, eds. *I Tell You Now: Autobiographical Essays by Native American Writers.* Lincoln: University of Nebraska Press, 1987.

Sweeney, Thomas W. "Fact Sheet." 2 August 1995. Washington, DC: U.S. Department of the Interior/Bureau of Indian Affairs.

Szabo, Joyce M. *Howling Wolf and the History of Ledger Art.* Albuquerque: University of New Mexico Press, 1994.

Taggett, Sherry Clayton, and Ted Schwarz. *Paintbrushes and Pistols: How the Taos Artists Sold the West.* Santa Fe: John Muir Publications, 1990.

Thom, Ian M., ed. *Robert Davidson: Eagle of the Dawn.* Seattle: University of Washington Press, 1993.

Thompson, Gregory C. "John D. C. Atkins." In Kvasnicka and Viola, *The Commissioners,* 1979, pp. 181–88.

"300,000 Indians Sue Federal Government for Mismanaging Their Money." *Native American Rights Fund Legal Review* 21(2)(summer/fall 1996).

Trennert, Robert A. "Luke Lea." In Kvasnicka and Viola, *The Commissioners,* 1979, pp. 49–56.

——. "William Medill." In Kvasnicka and Viola, *The Commissioners,* 1979, pp. 29–40.

——. "Orlando Brown." In Kvasnicka and Viola, *The Commissioners,* 1979, pp. 41–48.

"Tribal Leaders Rip Budget Cuts." *Rocky Mountain News,* 24 August 1995, p. 10A.

Trimble, Stephen. *The People: Indians of the American Southwest.* Santa Fe: School of American Research Press, 1993.

Twain, Mark. *Roughing It.* Berkeley: University of California Press, 1993 [1872].

Underhill, Ruth. *Red Man's Religion.* Chicago and London: University of Chicago Press, 1965.

U.S. Department of Health and Human Services. *Chart Series Book.* Washington, DC: Public Health Service, 1988 (HE20.9409.988).

Viola, Herman J. "Thomas L. McKenney." In Kvasnicka and Viola, *The Commissioners,* 1979, pp. 1–8.

Vizenor, Gerald. "Crows Written on the Poplars: Autocrtitical Autobiographies." In Brian Swann and Arnold Krupat, eds., *I Tell You Now: Autobiographical Essays by Native American Writers.* Lincoln and London: University of Nebraska Press, 1987.

——. *Interior Landscapes: Autobiographical Myths and Metaphors.* Minneapolis: University of Minnesota Press, 1990.

Wade, Edwin L., ed. *The Arts of the North American Indian: Native Tradition in Evolution.* New York: Hudson Hills Press, 1986.

Waldman, Carl. *Encyclopedia of Native American Tribes.* New York: Facts on File Publications, 1988.

Warrior, Robert Allen. *Tribal Secrets: Recovering American Indian Intellectual Traditions.* Minneapolis: University of Minnesota Press, 1995.

Waters, Frank. *The Book of the Hopi.* New York: Viking Penguin, 1977 [1963].

——. *The Man Who Killed the Deer.* Athens, OH: Swallow Press/Ohio University Press, 1994 [1942].

——. *Masked Gods: Navajo and Pueblo Ceremonialism.* Athens, OH: Swallow Press/Ohio University Press, 1984 [1950].

——. *Mexico Mystique: The Coming Sixth World of Consciousness.* Chicago: Swallow Press, 1975.

——. *Pumpkin Seed Point: Being Within the Hopi.* Athens, OH: Swallow Press/Ohio University Press, 1969.

Welch, James. *Winter in the Blood.* New York: Harper and Row, 1974.

———. *The Death of Jim Loney.* New York: Harper and Row, 1979.

West, Richard W., Jr., Michel Waldberg, Anne Vitart, and George P. Horse Capture. *Robes of Splendor: Native American Painted Buffalo Hides.* New York: The New Press, 1993.

Whitacker, Alexander. *Good Newes from Virginia.* Quoted in Moses Gait Tyler, ed. *A History of American Literature, 1607–1765* (Ithaca, NY: Cornell University Press, 1949), pp. 41–43.

Whitman, Walt. "Passage to India." In Baym et al., *The Norton Anthology of American Literature.* 3rd ed., Vol. 2, New York, London: W. W. Norton and Co., 1989.

Wiget, Andrew. *Simon Ortiz.* Number 74 in the Western Writer's Series. Boise, ID: Boise State University, 1986.

Witt, David L. *The Taos Artists.* Colorado Springs, CO: Ewell Fine Arts Publications, 1992.

Wong, Hertha D. *Sending My Heart Back Across the Years: Tradition and Innovation in Native American Autobiography.* Oxford and New York: Oxford University Press, 1992.

Wyman, Leland C. "Navajo Ceremonial System." In William C. Sturtevant, ed., *Handbook of North American Indians,* vol. 10: *Southwest,* ed. Alfonso Ortiz (Washington, DC: Smithsonian Institution Press, 1983), pp. 536–57.

Index